The Archaeology of the
Second World War

The Archaeology of the Second World War

Uncovering Britain's Wartime Heritage

Gabriel Moshenska

First published in Great Britain in 2012 by
Pen & Sword Archaeology
an imprint of
Pen & Sword Books Ltd
47 Church Street
Barnsley
South Yorkshire
S70 2AS

ISBN 978 1 84884 641 8

Typeset in Ehrhardt by Phoenix Typesetting, Auldgirth, Dumfriesshire

Printed and bound in India by Replika Press Pvt. Ltd.

Pen & Sword Books Ltd incorporates the Imprints of Pen & Sword Aviation, Pen &
Sword Family History, Pen & Sword Maritime, Pen & Sword Military, Pen &
Sword Discovery, Wharncliffe Local History, Wharncliffe True Crime, Wharncliffe
Transport, Pen & Sword Select, Pen & Sword Military Classics, Leo Cooper, The
Praetorian Press, Remember When, Seaforth Publishing and Frontline Publishing

For a complete list of Pen & Sword titles please contact
PEN & SWORD BOOKS LIMITED
47 Church Street, Barnsley, South Yorkshire, S70 2AS, England
E-mail: enquiries@pen-and-sword.co.uk
Website: www.pen-and-sword.co.uk

Contents

This book is dedicated to my grandparents

Acknowledgements

This book is the result of many years of digging, studying, reading, chatting and arguing about Second World War archaeology, and along the way I have met and worked with many brilliant and dedicated people. I am grateful to my colleagues and friends who have volunteered to work on my excavations over the years, enduring mud, misery and the general public in return for little more than tea, cakes and my undying gratitude, including Sarah Dhanjal, Susan Holmes, Don Cooper, Andrew Coulson, Morag McBride, Jim Nelhams, Andy Agate, Guy Taylor, Hannah Page, Jo Ward and Sarah Doherty. I have also been fortunate to have been allowed to work on other people's Second World War excavations in a variety of roles: my gratitude to Andy Brockman, Faye Simpson, Roy Stephenson, Peter Doyle and Larry Babits. Other colleagues have been kind enough to share stories, datasets and images with me, and several have given me permission to reproduce their photographs: my thanks to Nick Catford, Guy Taylor, Nathalie Cohen, James Dixon, Emily Glass and Andy Brockman.

My knowledge and understanding of the Second World War and its archaeological remains have benefited enormously from conversations and correspondence with a number of scholars and experts in the field. I am very grateful to John Schofield, Wayne Cocroft, Adrian Myers, Gus Milne, Gilly Carr, Martin Brown, Rod Scott, Neil Faulkner, James Dixon, Ross Wilson, Jon Price and Alfredo González-Ruibal. My students on the MA course unit *Archaeologies of Modern Conflict* at UCL Institute of Archaeology have been inspirational, and their research project assignments have opened my eyes to the diversity of conflict heritage around the world. During my fieldwork on various Second World War sites I have been fortunate enough to have met many people who lived through the events that I was studying, and who were willing to share their stories with me and make their memories part of my research. Talking with these people and recording their memories has been an extraordinary privilege and a reminder of the importance of studying the Second World War while it is still a part of living memory.

Enormous thanks must also go to my family, who have fed my fascination with Second World War sites and artefacts, and who have been dragged around more museums than is probably reasonable – including some particularly remote aviation museums. Thanks in particular to my parents, who read through early versions of the chapters of this book and gave excellent feedback and advice. I am massively indebted to Maria, who put up with my late nights, exhaustion and general crabbiness during the last stages of writing.

A final, special, thanks goes to Nick Saunders, who has been badgering me to write this book for many years, provided advice and support, and chivvied me on when I was dispirited about the whole project.

Preface

Every year in the Christmas holidays my parents drive out from Brighton to Cuckmere Haven near Seaford to walk the footpath that trails along the base of the valley to the sea, past grazing sheep and children riding new bicycles. As a small and energetic child, I ran up and down the valley and explored the rabbit warrens, ponds and old bunkers that line its sides. A few years later I canoed part of the stream that meanders down the central plain, and saw the remains of deep ditches lined with concrete cubes stretching from one side of the valley to the other. Over the years, as my interest in the Second World War developed and I began to learn the history of the area, I came to understand Cuckmere Haven as a defended landscape, a valley utterly transformed by the preparations for the German invasion of Britain. Today, thanks to the work of volunteer researchers and amateur and professional archaeologists who have studied and recorded the site, I have been able to appreciate Cuckmere Haven not only as a part of my family tradition but as one of the best preserved Second World War defensive landscapes in the country and an archaeological treasure-trove.

Nestled between high chalk cliffs, Cuckmere Haven with its sheltered beach and wide, flat valley bottom is a perfect landing site for an invading army heading inland towards London. The first anti-invasion defences on the site were built in 1804 in response to the threat from Napoleon's army, while in the First World War the valley was used for training, and no doubt some of the trenches and ditches that criss-cross the hillsides date from this period. As the Second World War approached, the German military began to identify likely landing sites and Cuckmere Haven was allocated as a beaching spot for the 6th Mountain Division. Had the planned invasion ever taken place we now know what these troops would have faced as their landing craft approached the Sussex coast. Anti-tank guns high up on the hillsides would have opened fire before the troops had landed, and on the beaches they would have come under fire from machine guns and small-arms in pillboxes manned by 135 and 136 Infantry Brigades. Above the beaches the German soldiers would have found themselves in a minefield entangled in barbed wire. Tanks and other vehicles supporting the German advance would have met a wall of concrete blocks stretching from the top of one valley side to the other, and beyond this a network of wide, water-filled ditches blocking their advance. Any German troops who managed to fight their way past the barbed wire, mines, light and heavy gunfire, ditches, blocks and hidden pillboxes would have found themselves in a marshy valley bottom studded with peculiar structures including electric lights on poles hanging above pools of water. These were bombing decoys designed to resemble the nearby port of Newhaven as seen from the air at night-time, and thus to confuse the German Luftwaffe bombardiers into wasting their bombs on empty fields: another part of the militarised landscape of Cuckmere Haven.

As the threat of invasion faded, the drive to build ever-greater defences began to disappear, but troops remained to guard the most vulnerable spots against commando raids and other incursions. After the war the beaches and inland sites were cleared of mines and barbed wire, and most of the fittings were stripped out of the pillboxes. Defensive ditches were filled in so that the land could return to its peacetime agricultural uses. Pillboxes in inconvenient locations were pulled down, and the anti-invasion landscape of Britain began to fade into archaeology. It would be half a century before archaeologists turned their attention to Cuckmere Haven. In 1995 the Defence of Britain Project was established under the auspices of the Council for British Archaeology, and more than 600 volunteers set about recording the survival and states of preservation of Second World War sites around the country. By the time the project ended in 2002 more than 20,000 sites had been recorded, creating a database that will form the basis of all future research into the archaeology of the Second World War. In 2002 the Defence Areas Project began, using the data from the earlier study to identify places where entire anti-invasion landscapes had survived. This project identified Cuckmere Haven as 'perhaps the finest group of surviving coastal defence works, with pillboxes of differing types dug into the cliff sides, large anti-tank cubes, an anti-tank wall, and open sections of anti-tank ditch'. Through this work the archaeological remains at Cuckmere Haven have been recorded and assessed: in recent years the data from these surveys have been used to prevent damage to the site by flooding, and to carry out repairs on the pillboxes on the site to prevent their deterioration. On my annual visits to Cuckmere Haven I walk the line of the anti-tank ditch, clamber over the 'dragon's teeth' blocks, and explore the litter-strewn interiors of the gun emplacements and bunkers. Here and there I find names or initials cut into the concrete and dates – 1940, 1941 – that remind me of the men who built the defences and those who manned them through the dark months early in the war when invasion seemed imminent. There are still people alive today who remember the erection of anti-invasion defences along the British coastline, and some who manned them. The archaeology and the records of those remains will serve as a testimony to the wartime generation long after they have passed; the duty of archaeologists is to bring the traces of the Second World War to life again to illuminate the lives and experiences of the people who worked, fought and died among them.

Introduction

The Second World War in History, Archaeology and Memory

The Second World War is perhaps the single most important event in human history. The titanic forces of destruction and creation unleashed during the six years from 1939 to 1945 left their mark on every corner of the globe, and the ripples and echoes of these events continue to shape the modern world. The Second World War destroyed nations and empires and gave birth to new ones, redrawing the political map of the world. It hammered vast and venerable cities into rubble, killed more than sixty million people, and forced millions more into exile. Many of the technologies and innovations that emerged during the war remain central parts of our twenty-first-century lives, including jet aircraft, computers, synthetic materials, antibiotics and nuclear power.

The Second World War is also probably one of the most studied and best-known events in history – at least in parts. The global nature of the conflict and the enormous variety in individual and national experiences of the war mean that there is not, and never can be, one single definitive history of the Second World War. The war experience of a British soldier in North Africa was utterly different from that of a child in wartime Finland – or, indeed, from a British soldier in Burma. All the books on the Second World War piled in one great heap would make the largest library in the world – a mixture of memoirs, military histories, studies of specific technologies, biographies, light popular works and weighty scholarly tomes, all written in scores of different languages and published across the world. In a thousand years no one person could read all of these books, and yet every day more are added to this imaginary heap by writers who have uncovered hitherto unknown or unrecognised events, or discovered a new view on an old story. Amidst this heap are books by those who lived through the war and books by

1

those who shaped the events. Winston Churchill wrote a history of the Second World War in six volumes, declaring that 'History will be kind to me, for I intend to write it'. Most of the millions killed in the Second World War left behind no memoir or diary. It is on their behalf that historians and scholars have worked to piece together the stories that add to our total understanding of this astonishing period of history.

In the shadow of this heap of books it is fair to ask what, if anything, an archaeological approach to the Second World War can tell us that we did not already know? After all, many of those who lived through the war are still alive. The archives are stuffed with documents recording every tiny detail, and newspaper and photo archives provide a day-by-day record of the war from start to finish. Can archaeology add a new chapter, a new perspective or any new material to the formidable sum total of human knowledge of the Second World War? As an archaeologist specialising in the study of the Second World War, I am naturally inclined to say yes. In fact I will go further: archaeology has already contributed to our understanding of the war in new and exciting ways, and looks likely to do so for some time to come. Moreover, as the number of people who remember the war grows ever smaller, a greater burden is falling on the heritage of the war – the historic sites, the archives and the collections. Here the job of archaeologists as the stewards of the traces of the human past takes on a greater weight of responsibility.

Archaeologists working on the prehistoric past build our understanding of ancient societies based only on the fragments of material remains that they have left behind, and are forced to make educated guesses about a great many aspects of the past. However, a considerable number of archaeologists work on places and periods that have some historical texts surviving as well: even ancient Mesopotamia, Egypt and the Mayans left inscriptions, tablets and paperwork for archaeologists to study, and to improve their understanding of the physical remains. Scholars of later societies such as medieval Europe or eighteenth-century Africa often have vast amounts of documents to draw upon, yet still there are some things that only archaeology can reveal. The difference between archaeological and historical sources is partly a reflection of their creators: for most of human history the skills of reading and writing have been restricted to the political and religious elites. The everyday artefacts, homes and workplaces that archaeologists uncover tell us about the common people who would otherwise fall between the cracks of history.

For the small number of archaeologists who study the recent past – including the Second World War – there is a third source of information available alongside historical documents and archaeological materials: the memories of those who lived through the events in question. At virtually every Second World War site that I have excavated in Britain and abroad we have been able to trace people who remembered them in wartime, and who were able – with their stories – to add to our understanding of the sites in ways that neither the history nor the archaeology would be able to. Talking with these older people as they visited our excavations brought the muddy sites and dusty objects to life, and our visitors often remarked that their memories were more vividly and powerfully evoked by the familiar sights and smells.

In the past few years the last survivors of the First World War have passed away: there are now no longer any living witnesses to the trench warfare of the Western Front or any of the numerous fronts of that titanic conflict, and even the youngest veterans of the Second World War are now in their late eighties. However, the Second World War was a total war fought in cities as well as on battlefields, and many of those with first-hand memories of combat, bombing and violence were young children when the war ended. Thus it will be some time before the Second World War slips out of living memory, but for individual episodes there will be moments when the last survivors will be lost. This is a tipping-point in our understanding of the war, and those of us studying it today understand the burden of duty that we bear to future generations to gather and preserve as much knowledge as we can before it is lost.

What is Second World War Archaeology?

The Second World War falls outside what most people would consider the timeframe of archaeology, and for this reason it is worth explaining what I mean by 'archaeology' in this book: what it includes, how it is carried out, what its aims are and what it is useful for. First, it is important to deal with a common misconception: not all archaeology is under the ground, and not all archaeologists excavate with trowels and brushes. A great deal of work carried out by archaeologists today, whether for research, environmental monitoring or as a hobby, involves methods such as studying objects and materials held in museums or archives, recording buildings, surveying monuments and other features in the landscape, or using satellite images and geophysical data to map sites and large areas. Archaeology is a twenty-first-century science and archaeologists have a wide range of tools at our disposal to study and protect the physical remains of the past.

I define archaeology, in the broadest sense, as the study of the human past from its material remains. These remains, as I have already noted, are not only found buried under the ground. A study of Ancient Egyptian archaeology would not be restricted to the things that could be recovered from an excavation: it would also include surveys of ruined temples and the dusty remains of ancient cities, the study of Egyptian artefacts from previous excavations housed in the back-rooms of museums around the world, and a careful reading of texts transcribed and translated from ancient papyruses. In the archaeology of the Second World War in Britain a similar range of techniques and sources are used. Structures such as anti-aircraft gun emplacements, airfield control towers, prisoner of war camps and old armaments factories are routinely recorded using archaeological surveying techniques, to study their construction and also to record more intimate details such as the remains of original fittings, signs and graffiti. Surveys of standing structures also record the state of preservation of these buildings so that they can be restored or protected from the elements. Second World War archaeologists can also apply these techniques – used by most archaeologists to study buildings – to some of the larger artefacts of the war. As I show later in this book, researchers have used archaeological techniques to examine vintage aircraft and sunken ships, finding traces of their manufacture and use, and learning how to preserve them for the future.

In many cases the archaeological remains of the Second World War are deeply buried, difficult or dangerous to access. In these cases archaeologists can use a range of 'non-invasive' methods to survey the sites and discover the locations of remains. This is particularly common for underwater archaeology, where wrecks can be hard to locate within hundreds of thousands of square miles of ocean floor. The wreck of the *Bismarck*, sunk by the Royal Navy in May 1941, was located using sonar surveying technology, and studied in more detail using remote-controlled mini-submarines. Other non-invasive techniques used in

Second World War archaeology include ground-penetrating radar (GPR) used to locate deeply buried structures and objects such as the remains of crashed aircraft and escape tunnels dug by prisoners of war.

Of course, a great deal of Second World War archaeology does involve excavating, as a vast proportion of the artefacts and sites of the war were abandoned to the elements or deliberately buried to dispose of them, while others such as landmines and air raid shelters were located underground in the first place. Some sites such as Home Guard gun and mortar emplacements were located in shallow trenches for protection, and many were buried after the war or merely filled with rubbish or other waste materials. Excavating these and similar sites is often a grim task of cutting back nettles and thistles before digging into the layers of sweet-wrappers and empty bottles built up over decades. Archaeologists are accustomed to excavating rubbish tips – in the centuries before formal rubbish collections were established it was common to burn or bury your household waste, and these rubbish pits can reveal a great deal about the diets and everyday possessions of the people of the past. In the Second World War vast tent camps and virtual cities of temporary wooden huts sprang up all over the country to house troops in transit, prisoners of war, displaced persons and others. While these camps often left few traces behind for archaeologists to study, they almost all had latrines (which we would prefer not to excavate) and rubbish pits (which we are happy to). I have excavated rubbish tips at a prisoner of war camp that revealed literally thousands of artefacts from buttons and bottles to identity cards, razor blades, nail brushes, food tins and toothbrushes – *hundreds* of toothbrushes. These artefacts – not important enough to appear in histories and not memorable enough to be mentioned in interviews – throw a great deal of light on life in the camps, including what the prisoners ate (a great deal of tinned meat) and their considerable appetite for grooming products.

Some of the sites that have been studied by excavation are those that were deliberately located underground to protect or conceal them. Many public air raid shelters were buried or half-buried to provide extra protection from bombs and collapsing buildings, and in many cases the shelters were sealed up after the war and forgotten, making them almost as exciting and surprising to uncover as buried tombs in the Valley of the Kings. In most cases, however, the things that ended up buried were the result of the more violent aspects of war. The field of aviation archaeology has long relied on excavation to recover the remains of aircraft that crashed and most often disintegrated. In many air crashes fragments of the airframe remained on the surface of the ground while larger heavier components such as engines, guns and armour plate tended to sink deeper as they would have hit the ground with considerably greater force. In some cases the engines of crashed aircraft have been recovered from more than 10 metres below the ground – far deeper than most archaeologists ever dig, and requiring special safety measures to protect the excavators from being accidentally buried.

Yet another way in which Second World War archaeology is unlike other forms of archaeology is the risk that the object that you are excavating might suddenly explode. Most of the bombs used in the Second World War were designed to embed themselves deep in the ground before exploding, to maximise the damage caused to surrounding buildings. Most artillery shells – including anti-aircraft shells – were not designed to bury themselves but their aerodynamic shape meant that they often fell to earth and penetrated to a considerable depth. Both bombs and shells were designed to explode but for a number of reasons their fuses tended to have high failure rates, and a large number of unexploded bombs and shells had to be removed by the army from the craters where they landed. In practice many of the bombs that fell in wasteland or rivers or unnoticed in other areas could stay in place for years, even decades, while retaining their capacity to kill. The unexploded shells of the First World War battlefields – the 'iron harvest' – kill a number of farmers and bomb-disposal specialists every year. In the cities that suffered heavy bombing during the Second World War the recovery of bombs from construction sites is a common occurrence, with a considerable number being found during the construction of the 2012 London Olympic site, and recent detonations of Second World War bombs in France and Germany causing deaths and injuries. While it is rare for archaeologists to find bombs, it is not uncommon for Second World War sites to reveal bullets and even grenades, all of which present a real danger and should be treated as live, left untouched and reported to the police immediately. Alongside the bombs are the sites that they destroyed: the rubble and ruins of bombed or burnt buildings is a key part of Second World War archaeology, as buried within the ruins are the traces of everyday life in wartime. Many of these objects are normal everyday things: cutlery, clothing, knick-knacks and toys, but it is the context where they are found by the excavator in the ruins of a bombed house that makes them part of the archaeology of the Second World War.

While excavating and surveying are common aspects of archaeology, the study of the material remains of the past extends beyond objects found in the wild to things that are found, often hidden in plain sight, in homes and gardens around the country. At the end of the Second World War most people wanted to forget the years of hardship and fear and move forward, and many of the most common traces of the war in everyday life were destroyed with glee: the bonfires lit around the country to celebrate VE Day were fed with thousands of gas masks and other unwelcome reminders of the war ceremonially consigned to the flames. Despite this urge to purge the everyday reminders of war, most were not destroyed but rather put aside. Air raid wardens' helmets were dumped on the tops of cupboards, gas masks left in sheds, badges and armbands for various civil defence organisations such as the Women's Voluntary Service were stuffed to the backs of drawers or bundled into jars of buttons and loose change. In my research on the archaeology of the Second World War I have found an air raid shelter sign used to patch a gap in a fence, tin hats left in an attic, a Home Guard uniform bundled into an old trunk, and scores of assorted medals, badges, shrapnel, bullet casings and other souvenirs kept in old cigar boxes and envelopes by former children of the Blitz. To understand these artefacts and to place them within the history of the war requires a mind as much anthropological as archaeological. These tiny fragments of the past are traces of the war, but for the people who collected and kept them they are something more, as I have discovered whenever I have interviewed people about their memories of the war. In short, there are stories in things and there are things in stories, and these artefacts wherever they are found are part of the heritage of the Second World War.

As well as describing the different things and places that fall within the archaeology of the Second World War, it is worth asking what it is for. What is the aim or purpose of studying these remains? There is no single answer to that, of course, as everyone who comes to work on the remains of the war arrives with their own motivations and ideas, but there are a few key ideas that should be emphasised. The first is preservation: if we believe that the material traces of the Second World War are of value and significance today, then we should also be concerned with preserving them for future years. To do this we need to know where they are, how well preserved and protected they are, and what their conservation needs are likely to be for the foreseeable future. A very few sites are not in danger: the vast concrete Citadel on Horse Guards Parade off Whitehall, with concrete walls many metres thick, is unlikely to be demolished or fall apart any time soon. For the vast majority of sites there are much more immediate threats. Coastal erosion has destroyed a considerable amount of the anti-invasion defences erected around the country in the early years of the war, while waves and corrosion will eventually batter even the sturdiest of historic wartime shipwrecks into scrap iron. Many of the structures and sites built in wartime such as prisoner of war camps and army camps were never meant to last more than a few years, and the cheap flimsy materials of their construction mean that preserving them as museums or heritage sites often requires an intense and expensive programme of conservation.

Aside from preservation, a good reason to study the archaeology of the Second World War is for research, to fill the gaps in the historical record and to increase our understanding of the history of the war, whether in a specific locale or across the country as a whole. Closely linked to this is the most common motivation of all: curiosity, often combined with the fascination that the Second World War holds for many people (including myself) who were raised on a diet of Airfix kits and old war films such as *The Colditz Story*, *Mrs Miniver* and *In Which We Serve*. This fascination with the war has driven the creation of voluntary associations and study groups such as Subterranea Britannica, the Airfield Research Group and the Fortress Study Group. Members of these and similar groups carry out by far the greatest proportion of research, monitoring and archaeological survey of Second World War sites in Britain and their collective knowledge and experience is the most important resource for ensuring the continued protection and appreciation of wartime heritage.

Alongside the wealth of voluntary work by study groups and independent researchers, the greatest advances in Second World War archaeology in the last twenty years have come through a series of ambitious, large-scale recording projects that have sought to map Britain's wartime heritage so that it can be managed and protected. From 1986 to 2004 English Heritage undertook the Monuments Protection Programme, a systematic nationwide survey of archaeological sites.

Among the numerous categories of sites covered in this programme, including prehistoric stone monuments and medieval castles, were the remains of twentieth-century military and defensive sites. The resources created by this programme were used in the establishment of a more narrowly focused survey, the Defence of Britain Project mentioned earlier. From 1995 to 2002 this innovative project used the expertise of hundreds of amateur Second World War archaeologists, working voluntarily, to record more than 20,000 anti-invasion sites and other wartime relics around the country, identifying not only the locations and types of sites but also their state of preservation. The archive of the Defence of Britain Project is the most important resource available to Second World War archaeologists, and its value will only increase over time as more and more sites are lost. The Defence Areas Project, mentioned earlier in relation to Cuckmere Haven in Sussex, used the data from the Defence of Britain Project to study places where large concentrations of wartime remains could still be found, to see how they formed entire landscapes of defence against invasion. The result of all this work is that Britain's Second World War heritage is better understood, recorded and appreciated than that of virtually any other country in the world – but that is no reason for complacency. There are always more sites in need of protection and new and exciting things to discover.

Who are the archaeologists who study the remains of the Second World War? There are not many whose work focuses only on this particular period, but many more who have an interest in Britain's wartime heritage alongside other commitments. A very few, like me, work in universities and are able, alongside our own fieldwork and research, to teach Second World War archaeology to students and encourage their interests in the field. Others work for organisations such as English Heritage or in local government, with responsibilities for managing archaeological heritage and ensuring that important sites are recorded and protected. The vast majority of archaeological work in Britain is carried out by commercial archaeological units working as contractors for the construction industry. Building housing estates, airports and wind-farms often damages or destroys archaeological sites, and archaeologists working for these units excavate or record the sites prior to their destruction so that the artefacts and information that they contain can be saved. Companies such as Oxford Archaeology and Museum of London Archaeology have considerable experience of Second World

War sites, usually as part of larger projects that cover a wide sweep of history from the recent to the very distant past. Still the largest group of people taking part in the archaeology of the Second World War are not academic or professional archaeologists but amateur archaeologists, many with specific interests in sites such as airfields, bunkers or aircraft crash sites, and many others who study the range of different wartime sites in their local areas. Many of these archaeologists record their work in magazines and journals, on websites and blogs, and some write books to share their knowledge with a wider audience. Professional archaeologists have long since learned to appreciate the depth of knowledge and skills that amateur archaeologists possess, and the future of research and excavation is to a considerable extent in their hands. Alongside individuals and study groups, there is a growing interest in the heritage of the Second World War among a much wider range of people, including teachers, school students, local history and oral history groups. The school curriculum for history contains a great deal about the Second World War and particularly (for older primary school students) about the Home Front. For young people who are becoming interested in the Second World War archaeology is a great way to learn, and in many schools around the country traces of the war can still be found, including air raid shelters in basements and under playgrounds.

The Second World War is of universal interest, and archaeology is something that everyone can take part in. It makes sense to make Second World War archaeology open to all members of the community who are interested, so that young and old people can work and learn together and share their knowledge and memories. This is what I have tried to do in my own archaeological fieldwork.

People of Second World War Britain

At the outbreak of the Second World War Britain's archaeologists sought ways to help defeat the Nazis. Many of the most experienced ended up working for the RAF, as their experience in interpreting aerial photographs was invaluable: if you can spot the remains of a Neolithic monument from 30,000ft then you can also spot a tank disguised as a haystack. Some of the most prominent archaeologists of the time, such as Glyn Daniel, Dorothy Garrod and Stuart Piggott, worked for the RAF, many of them at RAF Medmenham in Buckinghamshire and others in India. The swashbuckling archaeologist Mortimer Wheeler had won a Military Cross as a young artillery officer in the First World War, and at the outbreak of the Second World War he formed his staff at the Museum of London into a reserve anti-aircraft unit. With his superlative organisational skills and natural leadership (as well as a thoroughly military moustache), he soon advanced through the ranks, and took part in the Battle of El Alamein. By 1943 he was a brigadier responsible for anti-aircraft artillery in the Allied invasion of Sicily, before the world of archaeology summoned him back and he was appointed Director-General of the Archaeological Survey of India. Wheeler's philosophy of archaeology, and one that I share, was that 'too often we dig up mere things, unrepentantly forgetful that our proper aim is to dig up people', and that archaeology must be 'seasoned with humanity'. My aim in this book has been to describe some of the more important parts of the archaeology of Second World War Britain while always keeping in mind the people behind the artefacts and monuments.

In the Second World War the British military fought the Axis Powers around the world with air battles over Malta and Germany; sea battles in Scandinavia, the mid-Atlantic and off the coast of South America; and land battles in North Africa, Europe and the Far East. The archaeology of Britain's war effort is scattered around the world, mingled with that of our allies and our opponents. This book focuses on the remains of the Second World War that are found in Britain itself, and inevitably these can only tell part of the story. With the exception of the Channel Islands, Britain was not invaded or occupied by the Nazis, and no combat with German forces took place in Britain with the exception of a short gunfight with the crew of a downed bomber, the anti-climactic Battle of Graveney Marsh. In short, the archaeology of Britain in the Second World War is one part of a much larger story, but one that needs to be told.

The Second World War in Britain has been called the 'People's War', and it is true that for the first time the British people found themselves on the front lines of a global conflict, with air warfare bringing the risk of death or injury into the lives of men, women and children. In this book I have used the stories embodied in the archaeological remains of the war to shed light on the people who lived in Britain during the war, to try to glimpse the past through their eyes. Inevitably in a single book this can only be a partial view: shelves of books have been written on subjects like aviation archaeology that I can only touch upon briefly, and I beg the reader's patience if a favourite subject has received only cursory attention. Equally, some of the greatest contributions to the war effort in Britain have left little or no trace in the archaeology, such as the clothing factories that shifted to manufacturing uniforms using the same equipment and employees, and then after the war shifted seamlessly back to their peacetime activities.

The chapters of this book focus on the traces of the war as it would have been viewed from different perspectives. Each chapter takes a part of the population of wartime Britain and examines the history of their wartime experiences and traces the archaeological remains that relate to them most closely. In this way I have tried to cover the greatest possible range of sites and artefacts while maintaining a connection to the real-life experience of the British people and their wartime guests. The chapter on the Home Guard provides insights into the service that numbered hundreds of thousands of men who, far from being the bumbling old men of *Dad's Army*, became a highly trained volunteer military force. The archaeological remains of the Home Guard include the mortar emplacements and anti-aircraft sites that they manned, and the hidden bases of the secret Auxiliary Units designed to form the foundation of a British Resistance after invasion. The chapter on the role of the merchant marine in the war effort highlights the remains of the war at sea both underwater and on land, where the docks that received the essential war materials arriving by sea became the Luftwaffe's most important target. Millions of children in wartime Britain experienced evacuation, bombing and hardship and many thousands were killed or injured. Their archaeology is found on the bombsites that they turned into playgrounds and in the war materials that they collected, traded or used as toys, including gas masks and anti-aircraft shell shrapnel. One of the less well known parts of Britain's wartime population comprised the hundreds of thousands of prisoners of war, German and Italian, who were held in camps and often worked in agriculture or industry, many of them for years after the war ended. The traces of their presence in Britain remain in the hundreds of camps that were used to house them around the country, and in some of these camps there survives evidence of escape attempts, including the so-called 'Welsh Great Escape' and the first escape tunnels dug by Franz von Werra, famously *The One That Got Away*. In terms of impact on the landscape, the construction of dozens of airfields around the country before and during the war has left a sizeable archaeological legacy. The chapter focused on RAF aircrew examines these sites as well as the other traces that they left on the landscape, including air crash sites, many of which are still being investigated by archaeologists today. Finally, in towns and cities across the country there are the remains of civil defence sites, including air raid shelters, a testimony to arguably the largest organisation in wartime Britain, the air raid warden service, with almost one and a half million voluntary and paid employees, men and women, who provided training and equipment for survival amidst the bombs and were first on the scene after a bomb had fallen. The traces of civil defence, including the thousands of air raid shelters hidden in parks and gardens around the country, are a testimony to the efforts made to keep Britain going as the bombs rained down.

These groups of people experienced the war in different ways but also shared a great deal in common. As we approach the edge of living memory of the Second World War we can still learn a great deal from talking to them, but the burden of memory will fall ever more heavily on the remains of war that survive in British towns and cities, in the countryside and around the coastlines, beneath the soil and beneath the seas. This book is an introduction to what survives, what stories it can tell, and why it matters.

Further Reading

Calder, Angus, *The People's War: Britain 1939–1945* (Pimlico, 1991)

Calder, Angus, *The Myth of the Blitz* (Pimlico, 1992)

Dobinson, Colin, *Fields of Deception: Britain's Bombing Decoys of World War II* (Methuen, 2000)

Doyle, Peter and Paul Evans, *The Home Front: British Wartime Memorabilia 1939–1945* (Crowood Press, 2007)

English Heritage, *Twentieth-Century Military Sites: Current Approaches to their Recording and Conservation* (English Heritage, 2003)

Foot, William, *The Battlefields that Nearly Were: Defended Britain 1940* (Tempus, 2006)

Lowry, Bernard (ed.), *20ᵗʰ Century Defences in Britain* (Council for British Archaeology, 1996)

Robertshaw, Andrew and David Kenyon, *Digging the Trenches: the Archaeology of the Western Front* (Pen & Sword, 2008)

Saunders, Nicholas J., *Killing Time: Archaeology of the First World War* (Sutton, 2007)
Schofield, John, *Combat Archaeology* (Duckworth, 2005)
Webster, Donovan, *Aftermath: the Remnants of War* (Vintage, 1996)

Useful Websites

www.bbc.co.uk/history/ww2peopleswar/

The BBC People's War website contains tens of thousands of stories by people who lived through the war, including those who fought and those on the Home Front. It is the most extraordinary archive of wartime memories and a unique resource for learning about the history of the Second World War.

www.britarch.ac.uk/cba/projects/dob/

This is the homepage of the Defence of Britain Project, including an overview of the project and links to the archive, held by the Archaeology Data Service. The archive is searchable by type of site, place and period.

Places to Visit

Imperial War Museum

The Imperial War Museum in Lambeth, London, holds an unmatched collection of artefacts, vehicles, weapons, artworks, archives and displays relating to modern warfare. Founded after the First World War, it contains considerable material relating to the Second World War and the Home Front, including the walk-through Blitz Experience featuring a bombed street and an air raid shelter. Free admission.

Imperial War Museum London
Lambeth Road
London
SE1 6HZ
www.iwm.org.uk/visits/iwm-london

Chapter 1

The Home Guard

'Here, then, is the opportunity for which so many of you have been waiting. Your loyal help, added to the arrangements which already exist, will make and keep our country safe.'

Anthony Eden.

In 1940, as the German army advanced across the Low Countries and France, it became increasingly clear that Britain faced imminent invasion. Many politicians, some senior officers and a considerable proportion of the general population in Britain began to discuss the value and necessity of arming and training a citizen militia to repel invasion by sea or air. In May 1940 the British Expeditionary Force in France retreated to Dunkirk and was evacuated by sea with considerable losses in men and equipment, leaving Britain on the front line facing the German forces. At that point the Home Guard, in its early guise as the Local Defence Volunteers or LDV, was barely two weeks old: a ragtag army of all ages with barely any uniforms, weapons, training or organisation. In December 1944 the Home Guard was stood down, and shortly afterwards disbanded. By this time, contrary to the widespread *Dad's Army* image, it had evolved into a highly trained, well organised military force manning anti-aircraft artillery, patrolling sensitive sites and guarding key infrastructure, freeing up tens of thousands of regular troops for service overseas. The Home Guard was credited with numerous aircraft destroyed, and of the one and a half million men who served in it, more than 1200 were killed in service between 1940 and 1944. Like so many aspects of Britain's wartime heritage, many or most traces of Home Guard sites and activities have been destroyed, but many still remain hidden or forgotten, waiting to be unearthed or recognised. In the 1990s the Defence of Britain Project tracked down and recorded hundreds of Home Guard sites across the country, creating a permanent record of what survives in the landscape. Based in South-East London, the Digging Dad's Army project run by archaeologist Andy Brockman has begun to provide a much more detailed view of Home Guard activity in a particular area, while also carrying out surveys and excavations on other Home Guard sites of national significance. At Coleshill House, the training centre for the secret Auxiliary Units, excavations are revealing more about this shadowy force that would have formed Britain's Resistance army in the event of an invasion. The archaeology of the Home Guard is a well established part of British conflict archaeology with the promise of unearthing new discoveries and forgotten stories of Britain's citizens at war.

Background

Even before the war broke out there were rumblings in the press about the formation of armed citizen defence forces, and as the war progressed through early 1940 these calls increased in number and volume. Politicians and the press discussed the rationale for arming the population or some parts of it; as in the First World War there was a growing interest in rifle clubs, and many individuals began to purchase firearms and hoard ammunition. These developments were observed with concern by the army, who foresaw amateur involvement interfering with organised resistance to invasion; meanwhile the government expressed concerns that some citizen militias might have revolutionary intentions. This was not too far-fetched: one of the most influential thinkers in this early period was the journalist Tom Wintringham, a military theorist and Marxist who had fought in the First World War and commanded the British Battalion of the International Brigade in the Spanish Civil War. Wintringham was determined to create an anti-Nazi guerrilla force in Britain resembling the Republican militias in Spain; in the event of invasion this force would plant bombs and booby-traps, cut throats, sabotage key installations and make the German troops' work decidedly difficult. Wintringham's training centre at Osterley Park is discussed in more detail below. Meanwhile around the country a number of small militia groups were formed independently, with some beginning armed patrols of coastal and various inland areas. It was in part to control these independent forces, and partly in response to overwhelming popular demand, that the Local Defence Volunteers (LDV) was formed in May 1940, following a consultation between the government and the army.

In the BBC's nine o'clock news bulletin on 14 May 1940 Secretary of State for War Anthony Eden announced the foundation of the LDV. At a time when news of the war was growing worse by the day, most of the country would have been listening to their wirelesses when Eden declared that 'The government has received countless enquiries from all over the kingdom from men of all ages who wish to do something for the defence of their country. Well, now is your opportunity.' He announced that men aged 17 to 65 not already serving in the armed forces could enrol in the LDV at police stations. The LDV would be given uniforms and weapons but would not be paid, and would be expected to continue in their regular employment. By the end of the broadcast many men were already pulling on their coats and heading for the nearest police station to sign up. Eden and others had expected more than a hundred thousand volunteers but the response was overwhelming: within a day more than 250,000 had signed up, and within a month the figure stood at 1.5 million.

This positive response presented a number of problems. First, there was a shortage of enrolment forms (a sign of shortages to come) and many were signed up on the backs of envelopes and scrap paper. The overwhelming number of volunteers also exposed the lack of official administrative preparedness, as a regional command structure had to be improvised based around the offices of Lord Lieutenants and local army regiments. The promised uniforms and weapons were in many cases a long time coming, and for a time many LDV units paraded in civilian clothes and an LDV armband, and carried a range of improvised or dummy weapons. Among the LDV volunteers were a large number of First World War veterans – up to 40 per cent of the total force. There were also younger men in reserved occupations, such as arms industries, and older retired men, some of whom lied about their age to allow them to enrol. There was no formal medical requirement beyond the ability to walk, and no former experience of weapons or military training was expected. In London an LDV unit of American expats was formed, and many workplaces formed units of their own. More than 100,000 railway employees signed up, most guarding the parts of the railway infrastructure where they worked. Membership of the LDV often cut across social boundaries and brought together very diverse members of local communities – there are reports of retired generals serving as private soldiers in LDV units, and poachers serving alongside gamekeepers, while many MPs and peers signed up for the Westminster units.

Shortly after the formation of the LDV, Operation Dynamo, the evacuation of the British Expeditionary Force from Dunkirk, took place: 50,000 men of the regular army were taken prisoner and the army lost huge amounts of equipment, including most of its artillery and tanks, and large quantities of automatic weapons and rifles. Invasion seemed closer than ever, but the LDV remained under-equipped and under-prepared. Although most LDVs had been initially content to parade with only an armband to signify their role, the demand for uniforms grew. These arrived haphazardly and without much coordination: the first shipments were mostly denim overalls usually worn by the regular forces for carrying out dirty work. Shipments of denim trousers and jackets were sent out, often only one or the other, and often in odd sizes; many found the fabric tenaciously resistant to adjustments. Steel helmets and boots were also in short supply, and arrived gradually throughout 1940. In these and other resources the armed forces necessarily took priority. The name 'Home Guard' as opposed to LDV was first used by Churchill in a radio broadcast and the term became popular. The LDV had become accustomed to mocking nicknames such as 'Look, Duck and Vanish', 'Long-Dentured Veterans' and 'Last Desperate Venture'. When in late July 1940 Churchill proposed changing the name formally to the Home Guard, the greatest objection was that over a million more armbands would be needed at a cost of some tens of thousands of pounds, but this was quickly dismissed and the new name was officially adopted.

Home Guard Weaponry

The shortage of weapons remained a problem. Early parades had seen shouldered golf-clubs and cricket bats alongside shotguns and a few privately owned rifles. One widely mocked innovation was the pike, formed of a breadknife lashed to a pole. Some units drilled with dummy rifles, and stories abound of weapons being scavenged from museum cases, theatre prop boxes and mantelpieces. Officers of the First World War had often retained their revolvers, and in rural areas there were more guns in private ownership. The shortage of rifles was exacerbated by the army's losses at Dunkirk, and to equip the Home Guard the government looked abroad to Canada and the USA at weapons that it had previously rejected. The US military sent 100,000 M1917 rifles that had been mothballed in 1918; when issued to the Home Guard these were marked with a red band to distinguish their .300 ammunition from the standard issue British .303. It was a fine distinction but one that could jam or damage the rifles. From Canada came a large shipment of Mark 3 Ross rifles, an accurate but fragile weapon using standard .303 ammunition. Alongside all these came a mass of rifles and shotguns donated by American organisations and individuals, comprising a dizzying variety of calibres and types. This motley collection of odd or anachronistic bullet types makes it easier for archaeologists to identify Home Guard activity.

In the absence of conventional weapons the Home Guard troops were encouraged to assemble or use less conventional and often improvised armaments, such as grenades. The most common type used was the 'Molotov Cocktail', a bottle of flammable liquids used with some success in the Spanish Civil War and by the Finns against the Soviets in 1939. Home Guard guidelines suggested scoring the bottle to ensure breakage, and filling it with a mixture of petrol, resin and tar to create a clinging, longer-burning fire upon ignition. A petrol-soaked rag was to be tied to the bottle and ignited before throwing. It was imagined that several of these used at close-quarters would be effective against the light tanks that most armies in 1940 possessed in large numbers. It was advised that after the first Molotov Cocktail had hit, the others could be thrown without first lighting them. A similar weapon developed later was the phosphorus grenade, a Molotov Cocktail with yellow phosphorus and raw rubber added, creating a cloud of toxic fumes as well as fire. These were manufactured for anti-tank use, and more than six million were distributed to Home Guard units. Other improvised grenades were based on sticks of gelignite with detonators and fuses attached. The most simple version was a basic blast grenade, but alternative versions placed the gelignite within a tin of shrapnel or inside a metal pipe to create deadly flying metal fragments with a much wider kill radius than a stick of gelignite alone. All of these types, including the petrol bombs, required lighting with a match prior to throwing: this was a problem in wet or windy conditions, but a solution was found by dipping the ends of the fuses in safety-match head solution so that they could be more easily ignited.

Alongside these improvised weapons there were more elaborate manufactured grenades, such as the standard Mills Bomb, a fragmentation grenade with an easily recognisable pineapple pattern on its cast-iron shell, and a firing lever held closed by a pin. These could be thrown up to 15 metres (less than their lethal range!) or fired over longer distances using specially adapted rifles. The Mills Bomb was a reliable, proven weapon that remained in service from the First World War into the 1980s. In comparison, the ST grenade (or Sticky Bomb) was an unreliable but innovative weapon that arose out of desperation in 1940 when it was realised that most of Britain's anti-tank artillery had been abandoned at Dunkirk. While the Mills Bombs and gelignite-based grenades were anti-personnel weapons, the Sticky Bomb, like the Molotov Cocktail, was primarily aimed at anti-tank use. The Sticky Bomb consisted of an adhesive-coated glass sphere containing nitro-glycerine, with a handle attached and a thin metal case around the charge. Pulling the first pin would remove the case, revealing the sticky sphere, which would (in theory) adhere to any surface that it was hit against with sufficient force to break the glass bulb. A second pin would then release the detonator after a few seconds. These grenades were intended to be used against tanks at close-quarters, and several million were produced for use by the Home Guard. In tests they were found to be ineffective against wet or dirty tanks, they failed to stick to vertical surfaces, and they proved difficult and often extremely dangerous to deploy. While they found some success in use in North Africa, it is perhaps fortunate that Sticky Bombs were not required to be used in any great quantity.

Throughout the Second World War the various departments of government responsible for the military were inundated by amateur inventors with more or less fanciful plans for death rays, rocket weapons, super-guns and so on. Some might well have made a contribution to the war effort, but most were wildly impractical, insanely expensive or violated one or more physical laws. A few made it into production, such as Barnes Wallis's bouncing bomb, and some of those which made it into production probably should not have. Among this latter category were several weapons issued to the Home Guard.

The Northover Projector was one such. Designed as a light anti-tank grenade launcher, and resembling a length of drainpipe mounted on a tripod, the Northover Projector was the brainchild of Robert Northover, himself an officer in the Home Guard. It used a small black-powder charge to propel a grenade (either a phosphorus grenade or a standard fragmentation grenade) to a range of up to 300 yards. The phosphorus grenade was most widely used as it was believed to be the most effective against tanks. A cap from a child's cap gun was used to ignite the propellant charge, adding to the Heath-Robinson feel of the whole device. While the Projector displayed a number of problems in use, it was relatively popular with Home Guards, who found ways of mounting it on trailers and in motorbike sidecars for added mobility. Around 19,000 were in use by Home Guards by mid-1941.

The Smith Gun was a similarly basic anti-tank weapon introduced in 1942. Designed by a retired army officer, the Smith Gun had a short 3in calibre barrel and fired anti-tank rounds to an effective range similar to that of the Northover Projector. The Smith Gun was unusual in that it was mounted on two large wheels and was tipped 90 degrees onto its side to fire, one of the wheels serving as a base and pivot for the gun. From this odd position anti-tank or anti-personnel projectiles could be fired. Around 4,000 of these odd weapons were produced, despite official scepticism and the risks they apparently posed to their operators. They remained in service with the Home Guard until the end the war.

One of the most effective of the novel weapons issued to the Home Guard was the Blacker Bombard, which has also left a significant and easily recognisable trace in the archaeological record. The Blacker Bombard was a spigot mortar firing a 20lb bomb to a range of around 100 yards. It was designed to be operated from a heavy mobile platform, but found greater application in fixed defensive positions as part of stop lines and airfield defences, and provided many Home Guard units with their most authentic-looking artillery installations. The typical Bombard emplacement was a circular trench with a concrete pedestal in the middle, on the top of which was a steel pivot pin for mounting and rotating the mortar. Dugouts in the sides of the circular emplacement allowed ammunition and other parts to be stored, and sometimes provided shelter for the crews. Thousands of Bombards were issued to Home Guard units and emplacements were dug in key defensive locations such as road junctions, bridges and railway stations. Several hundred of these sites were surveyed by the Defence of Britain Project and their conditions and locations recorded. In many cases, especially where the installation has been filled in with earth, the steel pivot pin is the only part visible, or easily locatable with a metal detector.

The widespread view of the Home Guard as a ramshackle troop armed with pitchforks bore some elements of truth in the early months of its operation when the lack of uniforms, weapons and training led to sloppy parades and chaotic over-enthusiasm. The dozen or more motorists shot dead by Home Guards running impromptu road-blocks in May–June 1940 were victims of this early disorganisation, but it was soon overcome with training and better management. In the years after 1940 the status and makeup of the Home Guard went through a number of revisions. Men over 60 were forced out and those over 50 restricted to less active roles. Formal connections were made with local regiments to facilitate cooperation, and proper military rank structures were introduced. As a more efficient military force the Home Guard was ready to take on a range of roles far beyond those that were first imagined for it.

The Roles of the Home Guard

There remains some dispute about what the intended function of the Home Guard was, not least as it varied over time. Historian S.P. Mackenzie has suggested that official concern about independent militias and other vigilantes led to the formation of the LDV as a way of satisfying public demand for action in a climate of fear whipped up in part by the press. Initially described mainly in terms of anti-paratrooper activities, in the aftermath of Dunkirk the role was broadened slightly to relieve the regular army of tasks such as sentry duties on key non-military sites. With regard to anti-invasion work, the widespread official view of the Home Guard was that their role would simply be to 'sit in a pillbox and shoot straight', as one senior officer described it. In fact the Home Guard took up a wide range of roles, often employing unusual or innovative methods.

Wintringham's Guerrilla Army

The idea of training the Home Guard as an effective irregular force was considered and rejected by government and the military in the planning stages, following requests from MPs and others that the citizenry in general should be armed against invasion. Among the voices arguing against the 'sit in a pillbox and shoot straight' vision of the Home Guard, the loudest and most authoritative was that of Tom Wintringham. A prominent member of the Communist Party in the 1920s and 1930s, Wintringham had served in the First World War and became fascinated with warfare; he was described as the only Marxist military expert of the era, writing on military doctrine for a range of left-wing publications. In 1936 he travelled to Spain to write about, and later fight in, the Spanish Civil War. As commander of the British Battalion of 15 International Brigade, he took part in the ill-fated Battle of Jarama, and was wounded several times during his service. On his return to Britain, and having fallen out with the Communist Party, Wintringham continued to work as a journalist for several publications including the *Daily Mirror* and *Picture Post*. It was for this magazine that he wrote several articles on the Home Guard in its early form, noting its potential as a people's army and arguing for better training and equipment. His experiences in Spain had shown him the potential for irregular guerrilla warfare and the abilities of a citizen force to resist invasion, and he saw many similarities between the Republican militias of Spain and the British Home Guard. His writings urging the government to 'ARM THE CITIZENS' brought a very positive response from many individual Home Guard members and a few more forward-thinking army officers.

In June 1940 Wintringham set about forming a training school for Home Guards to learn the basics of guerrilla warfare and modern warfare in general, based to a considerable extent on his own experiences in Spain. With the help of Edward Hulton, the owner of *Picture Post*, he gained permission from the Earl of Jersey to use Osterley Park in West London as a training centre for 'ungentlemanly warfare'. The staff of Osterley Park were an odd assortment of desperados and geniuses: the surrealist painter Roland Penrose taught students the principles of camouflage, while Boy Scout fieldcraft instructor Stanley White taught scouting. A number of Wintringham's comrades from Spain took part in the training: Canadian soldier of fortune Al 'Yank' Levy taught knife skills and sabotage, Hugh Slater taught anti-tank tactics, and several Basque miners taught the proper use of explosives. The future MP and alleged Soviet spy Wilfred Vernon devised experimental explosives, including innovative Molotov cocktails and home-made grenades.

The Osterley Park training school was never officially recognised by the Home Guard or the army, but the programme was well publicised in the media and the week-long training courses were soon filling up with around 250 men at a time travelling from around the country to learn bomb-making and throat-cutting from Wintringham's motley team. Alongside Home Guards taking the course were members of the regular army, including a number from the Brigade of Guards. The students practised urban warfare around disused farm buildings, blew up mocked-up tanks, and fired rifles at wooden model dive-bombers. Students studied the works of T.E. Lawrence, Liddell Hart, Orde Wingate and others, and read accounts of guerrilla fighting in Spain, China and Ireland.

Official distrust of Wintringham's gang of subversives grew throughout 1940, and MI5 began to investigate his team while the army and civil service looked for ways of closing him down. Eventually the Osterley Park school was taken over by the military, who removed most of the radical elements of the curriculum and transformed it into a conventional training centre with the drills and square-bashing that Wintringham had disdained. Several other schools were opened around the country to train Home Guards in the use of various weapons and tactics. While the spirit of the International Brigades had been banished from the Home Guard, Wintringham's influence continued through his writing, including the books *Armies of Free Men* and *New Ways of War* (both 1940) and *Guerrilla Warfare*, co-written with Yank Levy in 1941. A last trace of the influence of Osterley Park on the Home Guard can be seen in a 1969 episode of *Dad's Army*, in which the troops are trained in warfare by the eccentric Captain Rodrigues, a Spanish exile.

In 2010 an archaeological project was set up to examine the remains of Wintringham's training school at Osterley Park, which is now owned by the National Trust. To celebrate the seventieth anniversary of the opening of the school, a team led by the Digging Dad's Army group carried out geophysical surveys and trial trenching on the site. This project built on earlier work, including collaborations with a Spanish Civil War re-enactment group and interviews with Home Guard veterans. The site of the training area turned out to have been partially buried by later construction work in the area, and the two trenches excavated on the site by the archaeologists had to break through layers of hardcore to reach the wartime levels. Careful excavation revealed the remains of training trenches dug on the site in 1940 and used to train the troops in ambushes and other forms of attack. It is hoped that future excavations will reveal more about the training activities that took place there in the summer of 1940.

Watching and Waiting

After its initial *Dad's Army* teething stages, the Home Guard emerged as an efficient and well run military force able to take on numerous tasks from the regular army, freeing up troops for overseas service, but it also took on a number of distinctive and labour-intensive roles in anti-invasion defence, particularly in the early years of the war. Home Guards patrolled and kept watch over large stretches of coastline in key invasion areas and elsewhere; while likely landing sites were heavily defended by regular troops and innumerable structural defences, the Home Guard kept watch on East Anglian beaches, Scottish islands and other key points. Throughout the country, including in and around cities, Home Guard units kept watch for enemy parachutists in the air or on land, having been earnestly warned that paratroopers might arrive disguised as nuns, priests, women or in other unlikely guises. Thus vigilant guards were kept on moors and hills, fields and suburbs. In many rural areas (and some urban ones) the Home Guard raised mounted units made up of farmers and huntsmen patrolling on horseback. Some of these units received training in shooting from the saddle, and while their potential effectiveness against German armour is doubtful, they would have had an advantage over paratroopers in remote areas with little cover. Bicycle-mounted units were more common and provided mobility in street fighting, although the troop of fast-moving roller-skating dispatch riders trained up in 1940 seems like one of the stranger ideas of the war.

The expectation that invaders would most probably come by boat led to a number of waterborne Home Guard units keeping watch on waterways and key installations such as bridges, pumping houses and locks. These forces included the Upper Thames Patrol, which checked key vulnerable points or 'VPs' for sabotage, with similar units on the Trent and elsewhere. A few Home Guard units acquired vehicles such as armoured cars, and some improvised by welding sheet metal on to vans or tractors. The Woolwich Arsenal Home Guard reportedly had a tank – a derelict vehicle abandoned on a firing range that they restored to decent working order. This unit was reportedly one of the best armed in the country, with access through their work to the most up-to-date small-arms available.

A great deal of Home Guard activity in the early years of the war was devoted to manning pillboxes and other defences on the web of anti-invasion defences that stretched across the country, forming successive lines inland from the coast and concentric rings around London and other cities. Given their numbers and availability, the Home Guard troops were ideally suited to this policy of 'defence in depth', and were relied on to man their defences rapidly in the event of invasion. Their defences were the tank traps, ditches, dragon's teeth, road-blocks and other structural defences installed in 1940. Their weapons included improvised incendiary devices such as the flame trap and the flame fougasse, a drum of petrol with an explosive detonating charge buried in a roadside and detonated by remote control: more than 50,000 of these deadly booby-traps were installed in Britain and most of the detonator switches were manned by the Home Guard waiting for the Panzers to come rolling up the road.

Sites such as bridges and railway lines were often mined or prepared for mining by Royal Engineers, but it was anticipated that many of the actual detonations would be carried out by the Home Guard. Similarly sockets and stanchions for road-blocks were installed in thousands of sites, with the girders and RSJs needed to complete them held by the Home Guard for deployment in the face of advancing German forces. Large sections of the stop-lines around the country were in the hands of Home Guards with their reject rifles, improvised artillery and unstable petrol bombs.

The Archaeology of a Stop Line

Shooters Hill in south London formed part of London Stop Line Central, part of the defence of the capital. In the event of a German invasion force landing in Kent – one of the most likely arrival points – this road would have formed a direct route into London for the Panzers and troops of the German Blitzkrieg. The task of the army and the Home Guard would have been to hold back the German advance for as long as possible, inflicting as much damage as they could. The sites clustered around Shooters Hill, many of them manned by the Home Guard, give some idea of the defensive roles that they were intended to play in the event of invasion.

The study, survey and excavations of the sites on Shooters Hill, which at one point included one of *Time Team*'s traditional three-day digs, began with the records of the Defence of Britain Project. These initially indicated a spigot mortar emplacement and two road-blocks: hardly the most powerful of defences. However, a survey of wartime aerial photographs and interviews with Home Guard veterans revealed a greater number and range of defences; in fact, there were considerably more road-blocks than had been initially thought, and the nearby woods and other local topography would have forced the invading troops on to the road, where further weapons were waiting for them. In mid-1940 a flame fougasse was installed below the summit of the hill, hidden in a makeshift roadside building. This would have been fired by the Home Guard further up the hill, engulfing any advancing forces in burning petrol, which would have flowed back down the hill into the attacking force. Further up the hill was a better defended 'killing zone' with a pillbox adjacent to the pub, reportedly disguised as an off-licence; the outline of this pillbox, since removed, can still be seen on the external wall. Further along the road bombing trenches would have hidden Home Guard bomb-throwers and a spigot mortar emplacement. The latter was excavated and found to consist of a shuttered concrete plinth with a pivot pin attached, resting on a poured concrete floor and surrounded by a circular corrugated iron revetment supported by angle-iron stanchions. This emplacement would have been ideally placed to fire mortar rounds at forces on Shooters Hill from cover, and the gun team would have been supported by fire trenches nearby offering covering fire from small-arms.

The archaeological survey and excavation of the Home Guard's anti-invasion defences on Shooters Hill also revealed the civil defence and anti-aircraft infrastructure alongside it: a number of surviving air raid shelters were surveyed and excavated, including one built to a unique and unusual design. While many air raid shelters conformed to standard designs or patterns, many were built by contractors for private home-owners, often with a novel layout or interior. These air raid shelters are some of the most important untapped (and neglected) resources of Britain's home front heritage. Close to the summit of Shooters Hill the *Time Team* excavation uncovered the mooring site of a barrage balloon, one of the most familiar sights on the Second World War skyline. These large silver balloons were raised and lowered on steel cables attached to a lorry and tethered to concrete anchors in the ground. The purpose of the balloons was to trap or deter aircraft – the steel cables were capable of slicing the wing off a fast-moving craft – and, like the anti-aircraft artillery, they had the effect of forcing enemy aircraft to fly higher or further away, making it more difficult for them to approach key sites and installations. The site of the barrage balloon was also used in the First World War as the site for an anti-aircraft artillery post. The balloons were operated by the RAF, but the Shooters Hill area also offered an insight into another Home Guard activity from later in the war: their service as anti-aircraft gunners armed with a range of light and heavy weapons, including the remarkable and little-known Z-battery rockets.

Home Guard Anti-Aircraft Activities

As the threat of invasion receded in 1941, following the German invasion of the Soviet Union, there was a move towards training members of the Home Guard to operate a variety of sites then manned by the regular military. The intention was to free up trained servicemen for service overseas or in training for D-Day, and to make better use of the more than a million willing and unpaid volunteers of the Home Guard. Many of the coastal artillery batteries around the country were handed over to Home Guard troops, with ordnance transport and storage often kept safely in the hands of more experienced troops. One of the greatest contributions of Home Guard members was in manning anti-aircraft artillery, particularly during the more common night raids – a task that the part-time Home Guard, many of whom worked regular hours, were particularly suited to. By mid-1942 more than 11,000 Home Guards had been trained in the operation of anti-aircraft artillery, including the heavy 3.7- and 4.5-inch guns and the smaller Bofors and other light AA guns. By D-Day in 1944 around 140,000 Home Guards were serving in AA command in a variety of roles, some under the auspices of the Home Guard Independent Light Anti-Aircraft Troops.

Close to Shooters Hill there are the remains of a rare type of site manned by Home Guards: a Z-battery. These were installations for firing large numbers of rockets in synchrony at approaching aircraft, creating a devastating barrage of fire. The 3-inch 'unrotated projectile' (UP) rockets carried the same warhead as a 3.7-inch AA shell, and could reach an altitude of around 22,000ft. The rockets were launched from rather basic rail projectors operated by a team of two, and their simplicity made them ideal for Home Guard use. In most cases the Z-batteries consisted of sixty-four projectors arranged in a large square, with support buildings close by for ammunition storage, fire control and canteen facilities. The rocket projectors were labour intensive in use, with up to 178 men required to operate an entire site. Combined with a reduction in the size of AA command, it was natural that the Home Guard would make up the numbers of Z-battery operators on sites around the country. Home Guard units served in this and other anti-aircraft roles in ever-greater numbers until the force was stood down in late 1944.

Like many Second World War sites across the country, the Z-battery at Shooters Hill is no longer visible on the ground. The site's location was established from the study of a sequence of aerial photographs taken throughout the war years, and from extensive oral history interviews with surviving members of the Home Guard who manned the battery. A series of geophysical surveys of the site have failed to find clear traces of the remains of the battery, which, like many temporary wartime sites, left very little material below the surface as evidence of its presence. The aerial photographs did, however, reveal that after the removal of the Z-battery in 1944, the site was used as a prisoner of war (PoW) camp, number 1020. It is not yet known what traces of the camp, which mostly consisted of Nissen huts, are left to be found on the ground, but a series of sketches drawn by a prisoner show the interior of the camp in some detail. Like the other sites on Shooters Hill discussed above, this research has been led by local archaeologist Andy Brockman, whose research into the area and its remaining traces of Second World War heritage continues to bring more evidence to light. The wealth of sites and archaeological remains in this small area gives some idea of the amazing range and number of sites that await study or discovery across the country, that will no doubt puzzle and delight archaeologists for years to come.

Auxiliary Units

One of the strangest and most secret forces connected to the Home Guard comprised the shadowy Auxiliary Units. These small groups of volunteers were selected from local Home Guards and given special training and equipment, including cunningly disguised secret hideouts. The purpose of the Auxiliary Units was to remain apparently as ordinary civilians as the Germans advanced across Britain, and then to carry out acts of sabotage and guerrilla warfare behind German lines to disrupt their lines of communication and supply. In short, they would have formed the nuclei of a British Resistance army. With food and supplies for ten days or so, these units were not expected to survive long, and would have been shot on capture. It was hoped that by then they would have wreaked some havoc among the enemy's rear echelons with the explosives they had been given and trained to use.

The Auxiliary Units were founded in 1940, at the same time as the Home Guard was being raised, and were placed under the direction of Colin Gubbins, later head of the Special Operations Executive (SOE). Like SOE, the Auxiliary Units operated outside the main structures of the military and the Home Guard, and were run by a branch of military intelligence. Many details about the Auxiliary Units and their precise roles remain classified, with the records sealed until 2045. Like the Home Guard in general, the Auxiliary Units drew their membership from men of a range of ages and occupations, with an emphasis on game-keepers, poachers and others with a good knowledge of the landscape and field-crafts. Recruits were sworn to secrecy, and could not reveal their membership or activities to family or to the other Home Guards (although it remains doubtful whether they were actually counted as Home Guard members as they were led to believe).

The foundations of the Auxiliary Units' activities were their Operational Bases (OBs), clandestine dugouts hidden in the landscape with ingenious secret entrances and concealed viewing points. Each OB was connected to an Operational Patrol of up to eight men. Many of the bases, which numbered more than a thousand in total, were dug into remote hillsides and fields by army units operating in strict secrecy. If observed by passers-by, they were instructed to give false information about the purposes of the sites. The typical OB was a subterranean structure about the size of a caravan, built from wood and corrugated iron, and designed to hold six or seven men in no great comfort. Many were damp and poorly ventilated, but alongside storage for weapons and supplies they contained bunkbeds for the men as well as rudimentary cooking facilities and chemical toilets. While most bases were built from scratch, a few used existing structures such as disused cellars, caves, badger setts and mines. Most OBs had concealed entrances, many of them secured with elaborate systems of catches and switches.

In the post-war period most OBs were destroyed or sealed by the military to hide their existence, but in practice many have survived in some form. Auxiliary Unit sites were surveyed as part of the Defence of Britain Project, and several hundred sites of various kinds were reported, although this included the sites of several OBs that had been largely or completely destroyed. In many cases the OBs were discovered because of the collapse of part of the structure or one of the entrances, either because of work taking place above them or due to natural decay. The corrugated iron and wood (including logs) used in the construction of many OBs have also tended to degrade, and many of the surviving sites are at risk of further damage from water and time, as well as from vandalism or development, although some are no doubt protected by their remote locations. It is in the nature of secret sites that some or even many OBs probably remain undiscovered and unknown, possibly including some of the best preserved.

The Auxiliary Units were given training in weapons, fighting, field-crafts and demolition at a secret training centre at Coleshill House, Wiltshire, chosen for its remoteness by Colin Gubbins. Training aids at the site included working and derelict vehicles and aircraft remnants used for sabotage and demolition training, and a mock-up OB for practice. Staff and trainees stayed in the house, its outbuildings and in Nissen huts in the grounds. Parts of the site of Coleshill House have been surveyed and excavated to trace the remains of the training facilities. A number of Nissen hut bases have been uncovered, and finds from the hidden OB include a bayonet concealed behind a false wall, several bullet cases, grenade fragments and a live mortar bomb that had to be destroyed by a bomb-disposal team (a reminder of the hazards of conflict archaeology and the need for caution on sites that might contain such hazardous materials!). The archaeology of Auxiliary Unit training at Coleshill House and the traces of OBs in the landscape tell one of the strangest and least-known stories of citizen soldiers in the Second World War.

Summary

From its *Dad's Army* beginning as the LDV marching with makeshift pikes to defend Britain's coastline from invaders, the Home Guard evolved into a large and effective military force serving in a number of vital roles in wartime Britain. Whether guarding railway junctions, manning guns on coastal batteries or anti-aircraft units, or keeping guard on lonely cliff-tops, the Home Guard formed a key component of Britain's war effort. Like so much of Britain's wartime heritage, much of the archaeology of the Home Guard is the record of defences against threats that never materialised. The German invasion barges never sailed across the Channel and paratroopers never fell silently onto remote moors. Had they done so, their Panzers would have been met by the improvised artillery and unstable petrol-weapons of the Home Guards manning stop-lines, and the parachutists would have been challenged by men armed with automatic weapons as well as pitchforks and stout sticks. It would be wrong to let this frustrated potential devalue the sites and artefacts of the Home Guard's war, and the archaeological projects now probing the spigot mortar emplacements and Auxiliary Unit hidden bases around the country will, it is hoped, help to bring their story into the light.

Further Reading

Carroll, David, *The Home Guard* (Sutton, 1999)

Cullen, Stephen, *In Search of the Real Dad's Army: the Home Guard and the Defence of the United Kingdom 1940–1944* (Pen & Sword, 2011)

Dobinson, Colin, *AA Command: Britain's Anti-Aircraft Defences of the Second World War* (Methuen, 2001)

Foot, William, *Beaches, Fields, Streets and Hills: the Anti-Invasion Landscapes of England, 1940* (Council for British Archaeology, 2006)

Longmate, Norman, *The Real Dad's Army: the Story of the Home Guard* (Amberley, 2010)

Lowry, Bernard, *British Home Defences 1940–45* (Osprey, 2004)

Mackenzie, S.P., *The Home Guard: a Military and Political History* (Oxford University Press, 1995)

Purcell, Hugh, *The Last English Revolutionary: Tom Wintringham 1898–1949* (Sutton, 2004)

Storey, Neil, *The Home Guard* (Shire, 2009)

Warwicker, John, *Churchill's Underground Army: a History of the Auxiliary Units in World War II* (Frontline, 2008)

Useful Websites

www.home-guard.org.uk

This site provides a variety of information on the history of the Home Guard and its equipment, and is linked to the Chatham Home Guard living history group.

www.auxunit.org.uk

A website devoted to the history of the Auxiliary Units, including personal stories and details of Auxiliary Unit equipment and operational bases.

www.coleshillhouse.com

Coleshill House was the training centre for the Auxiliary Units, and this site exhibits the work of the Coleshill Auxiliary Research Team.

Chapter 2

The Merchant Mariner

In the early morning of 8 April 1942 the oil tanker SS *Esso Baton Rouge* was hit by a torpedo from U-boat *U-123*, and settled in 7 fathoms of water off the coast of Georgia, USA. Three members of the crew were killed in the explosion, including the Second Assistant Engineer, James Eagan Layne. *Esso Baton Rouge* was refloated and served for another year before being torpedoed for a second and final time in a convoy bound for Curacao. On 2 December 1944 a Liberty Ship named SS *James Eagan Layne* was launched in New Orleans by Layne's widow; it was one of 2,710 Liberty Ships built during the Second World War, and the first to be named after a merchant seaman killed in the war. In March 1945 SS *James Eagan Layne* was part of Convoy BTC-103 from Wales to Belgium, carrying military supplies, when it was torpedoed by *U-399*. The torpedo struck on the starboard side, behind the bulkhead separating holds 4 and 5, damaging the hull, rudder and propeller. The crew evacuated without injury, and the ship – which refused, at first, to sink – was taken under tow into Plymouth but grounded to the west of the port, settling in around 20 metres of water with parts of its super-structure protruding from the surface.

Of the tens of thousands of shipwrecks that line the British coastline, many hundreds date to the Second World War, when German U-boats and mines took a heavy toll on British, allied and neutral shipping. SS *James Eagan Layne* is just one among these thousands, but for explorers of underwater heritage it is more than just a statistic. Located in shallow water close to Plymouth, it has become the most popular wreck for scuba-divers in Britain, from the early days of the sport in the 1950s up to the present. Over the years the wreck has begun to decay, and has become an artificial reef for sea-life as well as a focus for recreational diving. Most of the divers who explore the wreck learn something of its history, and many come to learn a great deal about the role of the Liberty Ships and other vessels in the convoys that kept Britain supplied with food, fuel, war materials and other essentials during the Second World War. As an island nation, it was inevitable that the war at sea would become a vital front in the wider conflict, and much of the archaeological heritage of the Second World War is to be found in and around ports and docks, as well as beneath the waves of British waters. In this chapter I will look at the surviving traces of the Battle of the Atlantic and the U-boat war, both at sea and in British ports.

For much of recent history the movement of goods by sea and the military control and protection of the sea trade has been a fundamental part of Britain's prosperity and security. Both in peace and in war Britain has depended on imports of fuel, food, raw materials and other commodities to survive. London's role at the heart of the Empire was proven by the goods from around the world that flowed in and out of the Port of London – for a long time the largest and busiest port in the world. As a maritime nation, Britain's port cities became large employers of dockers, shipwrights and associated professions, and the industrial revolution was fuelled in part by the coal carried from mining towns to industrial towns by sea and canals in British-built vessels. In light of this nautical dependency and supremacy, it was only natural that in the First World War the German navy would attempt to starve Britain of arms and food by torpedoing its ships and bombing its port cities, but it was the more effective British naval blockade of Germany, as much as any battlefield triumph, that ultimately decided the war.

In the Second World War Nazi Germany again attempted to limit Britain's ability to fight by harrying the lines of supply that stretched from around the world into British ports. The Battle of the Atlantic, fought between Allied shipping and German warships, as well as aircraft of both sides, became the longest-running front of the entire conflict, with considerable losses on both sides. It was also, like the air war, a conflict of technological supremacy with rapid advancements in radar, radar-countermeasures and other resources, including most famously the 'Ultra' signals intelligence gathered by the code-breakers of Bletchley Park that offered the Allies an inside-view of the German military machine. Alongside the Battle of the Atlantic there was the Blitz – or, more precisely, the Blitzes – as ports and shipbuilding areas around the country from Southampton to Clydeside came under heavy air attack throughout late 1940 and into 1941, as well as intermittently throughout the rest of the war.

Throughout this battle at sea, on land and in the air, a considerable proportion of the combatants on the front lines were not servicemen but civilians – merchant mariners and dockers. The former served alongside (and sometimes on the same vessels as) men of the Royal Navy as well as the American, Canadian and other commonwealth navies. Above the convoys the aircraft of RAF Coastal Command hunted U-boats and mounted a watch. In the ports and shipyards the dockers, welders and riveters (many of the latter women) worked under the protection of army and Home Guard anti-aircraft gunners, RAF balloon crews, and fire and rescue crews both regular and voluntary. In the total war of the Battle of the Atlantic and the Blitz, all of these people shared the dangers of the front line, as witnessed in the coral-coated wrecks and burnt remains of wharves around the country.

Alongside the divers and archaeologists studying Britain's underwater heritage of the Second World War there are numerous historical and heritage organisations devoted to the study and commemoration of the docks and shipyards that formed the British front line of this battle. Museums in Liverpool and Glasgow as well as national naval and maritime museums hold collections including historic vessels, and some are housed in original dockyards and warehouses. On the Thames there is HMS *Belfast*, a light cruiser that served as a convoy escort during the war. Along the foreshore of the Thames tideway a community archaeology and history project – the Thames Discovery Programme – has recorded (and continues to monitor) a huge amount of information about the history of the Thames, including a considerable amount that relates to the Second World War, much of it hitherto hidden or forgotten.

The War at Sea

On 3 September 1939, the day that Britain entered the Second World War, U-boat *U-30* fired two torpedoes at SS *Athenia*, an unarmed British liner en route to Montreal with 1,400 passengers and crew. One torpedo malfunctioned but the other hit the liner and exploded, causing her to begin to sink. This incident off the north-west coast of Ireland marked the first attack on a British ship in the Second World War and a day later, when *Athenia* finally sank, the first casualties. More than a hundred people were killed in the attack and its aftermath, although most of those on board were rescued by nearby ships. Under international law, and under the German navy's rules of engagement, the attack was illegal, and the Kriegsmarine was forced to effect a cover-up. With this inglorious engagement the Battle of the Atlantic began – a battle that would last almost the entire duration of the Second World War.

Mines

For the British the early months of the war are often described as the 'phoney war', in which little fighting or bombing took place. While this may have been true for the population in general, and for many in the army and air force, it was not true of the war at sea which was a 'hot' war from the very beginning. From September 1939 the German navy and the Luftwaffe deployed hundreds of mines in the Thames estuary to disrupt shipping into the Port of London. Many of these were magnetic mines, detonated not by contact but by a vessel's magnetic field. One of these mines, accidentally dropped onto land, was recovered by the army and subjected to tests, leading to the development of an effective countermeasure – just one of many technological advances in the tit-for-tat game of military innovation that characterised the war at sea. By the time the magnetic mines had been beaten, several hundred ships had already been lost, many of them in the Thames Estuary – a frustrating loss of men, vessels and cargoes so close to home, often after a journey of thousands of miles through enemy-infested waters. The mining of ports, sea-routes and naval bases with air-dropped and sea-laid mines was practised by both the British and the Germans in this period, with varying degrees of success. A distinctive set of survivors of this period of the war are the Maunsell Sea Forts – anti-aircraft gun emplacements on concrete towers or legs, placed miles out to sea in the Thames and Mersey Estuaries and equipped with heavy and medium artillery to deter or destroy mine-laying aircraft. Some enjoyed a brief after-life as bases for pirate radio stations, and one surviving fort is now the self-declared Principality of Sealand – a tiny independent 'nation'. Another remnant of the mining campaign is the small number of surviving mine-watchers' posts – small pillboxes with viewing windows. These posts would be arranged in groups of two or more, and mines dropped by parachute were plotted onto maps by the spotters, using triangulation between the posts. Several surviving mine-watchers' posts are recorded in the Defence of Britain Project database in Pembrokeshire and elsewhere. The Thames Discovery Programme recorded a mine-watchers' post at Tripcock Ness – an unusual example covered in a layer of 'plastic armour' – rough tarmac – more commonly used as defensive armour on the superstructures of armed merchant ships.

U-boats

Perhaps the most iconic weapon of the war at sea was the German U-boat, with its fearsome reputation earned in the First World War. At the outbreak of war the German Kriegsmarine possessed more than sixty U-boats, and over the course of the war approximately 1,150 were commissioned, more than half of which were lost in action – a very high rate of attrition. The most common U-boat was the Type VII, of which more than 700 were built before and during the war. These formed the backbone of Admiral Karl Dönitz's submarine force, with most operating in the Atlantic. The Type VII was 67 metres long, with a crew of around fifty, and was armed with torpedoes and a formidable deck gun. Like most U-boats, it had two power sources: a diesel engine for use on the surface, and an electric motor for use when submerged, with batteries charged by the diesel engine. The Type VII was capable of speeds of up to 18 knots on the surface, but less than 8 knots submerged. In many respects the majority of German U-boats in the Second World War served as surface torpedo boats, patrolling on the surface and carrying out many of their attacks while surfaced, particularly at night.

Early in the war the Kriegsmarine developed the 'wolf-pack' system whereby U-boats would assemble in groups around a convoy, located by aerial reconnaissance or signals intelligence, and would attack together, making it harder for the convoy escorts to counter-attack. This strategy proved successful and in the early years of the war several hundred Allied ships were lost in the Atlantic. Before the introduction of adequate air cover and radar-equipped destroyers, the mid-Atlantic was a vulnerable area for convoys and a safe hunting ground for U-boats, whose crews referred to this period in retrospect as the 'Happy Time' of the war at sea. After the fall of France, the U-boats were able to operate out of ports on the west coast of France, making it much easier for them to reach the mid-Atlantic without passing through the Channel or round the north of Britain. The massive concrete U-boat pens at Lorient and elsewhere are a lasting reminder of this period. Built from hundreds of thousands of tons of reinforced concrete, the vast covered docks and dry-docks allowed the Kriegsmarine to repair and refit its U-boats while protected from Allied bombs by a roof up to 7 metres thick. Only towards the end of the war would these bases become vulnerable, as the RAF developed the 12,000lb Tallboy and 22,000lb Grand Slam earthquake bombs, capable of piercing the reinforced concrete roofs of the U-boat pens then under construction in Bremen and elsewhere. Due to their size and strength, most of the U-boat pens built during the war can still be seen today, with some, such as the Valentin bunker in Bremen, becoming memorial museums.

As the war progressed, the high shipping losses threatened to weaken Britain's ability to fight, and Churchill expressed serious concerns about the U-boat threat. An arms race began, as new technologies were introduced to enable convoy escorts and other naval vessels to locate and destroy the U-boats. These included new means of detection, new offensive weapons and new sources of intelligence. From 1941 escort vessels and some maritime patrol aircraft began to be equipped with radar that could detect U-boats on the surface. While some U-boats were equipped with radar detectors that could warn them of an imminent attack, these were soon ineffective against the new shorter-wave radar. Allied vessels began to use radar together with sonar and a variety of anti-submarine weapons, including depth-charges and 'hedgehog' and 'squid' mortars. The hedgehog was based on the Blacker Bombard, a spigot mortar used mainly by the Home Guard. The squid mortar, linked directly to the sonar, was an early example of an automated weapons system, and indicates the degree of innovation and inventiveness that went into the arms race on, above and below the Atlantic.

Under constant attack from both aircraft and warships using radar, rockets and depth-charges, and from mines, the U-boat forces of the Kriegsmarine saw the Battle of the Atlantic turn against them. At the war's end the surviving U-boats surrendered to the Allied forces, with many of them being held at Lisahally in Northern Ireland, a centre of anti-submarine warfare during the war. In 1945 and 1946 116 of these captured U-boats were sunk off the northern coast of Ireland in Operation Deadlight, although many sank at sea on their way to the pre-arranged sinking site. These vessels, resting in around 70 metres of water, are a lasting reminder of the Battle of the Atlantic and a key maritime archaeological resource. In 2007 a plan was mooted to raise one of the U-boats that sank off Malin Point and place it in a museum in Derry. A similar campaign in 1993 raised *U-534* from the bottom of the North Sea, in the hope of finding a treasure cargo of gold. This proved elusive, however, and *U-534* was ultimately put on display in Merseyside, in part as a memorial museum to the Atlantic convoys and the Battle of the Atlantic.

While most U-boat wrecks are located in European waters or in the eastern Atlantic, one notable wreck was discovered by maritime archae-ologists in 1991 off the coast of New Jersey in the US. Discovered hundreds of miles from any known U-boat sinking site, this mystery vessel presented a conundrum for investigators. A deep and dangerous wreck site that has claimed the lives of several divers, it was finally identified as *U-869*, captained by Hellmut Neuerburg, and previously thought to have been sunk off Gibraltar. Explorations of the wreck found that it still contains the bones of its crew, a grim reminder of the human cost of the Battle of the Atlantic and a reminder to archaeologists that the sites we investigate are often also war graves.

Breaking the Codes

Perhaps the most important front in the Battle of the Atlantic was fought not at sea but in the airwaves, as the wolf-packs of U-boats radioed the locations of convoys to one another and received directions and orders from their home bases. These coded messages were routinely inter-cepted and passed to code-breakers to decipher. Their success or failure in decoding the German transmissions might have meant the difference between a convoy's survival or its destruction. Over the course of the entire war the code-breakers' activities helped to shape the outcome of the conflict.

The front line of the battle of the codes was a country house in Buckinghamshire. Bletchley Park housed the Government Code & Cypher School, where teams of code-breakers worked in temporary huts and outbuildings to decipher the various German codes. The Kriegsmarine code was the most secure, using the hi-tech Enigma machines, although this apparent security meant that the operators were more confident in sending longer and more detailed messages. Through careful study of the codes, errors made by the Enigma operators and ingenious technological innovations, the Enigma codes were broken and Allied naval intelligence was able to direct their convoys to avoid the U-boat wolf-packs and their warships and aircraft to attack them. In several of these naval interceptions of U-boats in the early years of the war Enigma machines and code-books were captured, providing the final pieces of the puzzle for the code-breakers at Bletchley. The measure of the success and the impact of the code-breakers' work came in 1942, when the Kriegsmarine introduced a new, more complicated version of the Enigma machine and allied shipping losses climbed sharply for almost a year until this code was also broken.

Today Bletchley Park is a heritage site and museum, renowned not only as a part of Second World War history but also as the birthplace of the digital computer, developed in a variety of forms by scientists and mathematicians, including Alan Turing. The Bletchley Park site grew in the course of the Second World War to house a staff of around 10,000. Many of these people were based in a large array of outbuildings, wooden huts and other temporary buildings around the main house, which appeared gradually over the course of the war. Many of these buildings were not constructed with long-term use in mind, and the problems of preservation have made Bletchley Park an expensive heritage site to keep for posterity. Nevertheless work by English Heritage archaeologists has recorded the site in considerable detail and it is hoped that it will remain as a museum to one of the most extra-ordinary and vital parts of the Second World War in Britain and beyond – a story that was kept secret for decades after the war's end.

One piece of the archaeology of code-breaking has been revealed as a deliberate myth. It was long believed that the vast electronic computers constructed at Bletchley Park, the first digital computers in the world, were broken up at the end of the war. According to the myth, the computers were demolished and buried in pits on the site – a fascinating opportunity for archaeologists to explore this historically important material. In fact the story of demolition and burial was a smokescreen – the computers were, in fact, transferred to the government's new intelligence site at GCHQ.

Liberty Ships

The British merchant mariner of 1939 most likely served on one of the thousands of vessels – almost one-third of the world's merchant fleet – that sailed under a British flag. Many of them were the products of the shipbuilding industries of the Tyne, Tees and Clyde, and their crews included men from all parts of the British Empire and beyond. The staggering losses that they suffered from the outbreak of the war onwards meant that replacements were desperately needed, a problem compounded by the steady erosion of the British shipbuilding industry since the end of the First World War, and the resulting impoverishment of several major industrial areas.

While British shipbuilders struggled to replace the lost vessels, orders were placed with shipyards in the US and Canada to build substantial quantities of ships for the convoys. A new design was needed to meet the unprecedented demand from British shipping companies for 10,000-ton vessels. In the 1930s the Sunderland shipbuilders J. L. Thompson & Sons had created a pioneering design for a simple and reliable cargo ship, and a modified version of this design became the basis of this manufacturing boom. While different versions of the design were created under various names by shipyards in the US and Canada, the best-known name for these vessels – based on a remark by President Roosevelt – was Liberty Ships.

The 135 metre-long Liberty Ship was built using an innovative modular method, and notably made use of welding rather than riveting for most of the construction. Using these time- and labour-saving methods, by the end of production the average time from laying the keel to launching was little more than a month. The propulsion came from simple and reliable reciprocating steam engines, of around 2500hp, pushing the Liberty Ships to a maximum speed of around 11 knots. These unattractive but practical vessels carried a maximum load in the region of 10,000 long tons in holds fore and aft of the centrally located bridge structure. The crew numbers varied between forty and eighty, including military personnel to operate the ship's defensive armament. Most Liberty Ships carried a stern-mounted gun of around 4-inch calibre, often obsolete naval guns, for use against surfaced U-boats. Most also carried anti-aircraft machine guns or cannon for use against low-flying attackers. With this armament in place, the Liberty

Ship was classed as a DEMS – a Defensively Equipped Merchant Ship.

Of the 2,700 Liberty Ships, and the hundreds built in Canada to similar designs, many fell casualty to U-boats, aircraft, mines and other perils. However, a significant number of the Liberty Ships that lie wrecked beneath the seas were sunk by structural failures. The speed of construction and the variations in build quality between shipyards meant that some Liberty Ships were prone to cracking, and in some cases even to breaking in half along poor weld lines. Moreover, it was soon discovered that some of the most catastrophic structural failures were due to the poor quality of the steel used by some shipyards.

The most famous Liberty Ship wreck in British waters is undoubtedly SS *James Eagan Lane*, mentioned earlier, but SS *Richard Montgomery* is likely a close second, and offers an alarming illustration of the risks that the heritage of the Second World War can pose to contemporary Britain. In August 1944 SS *Richard Montgomery* sailed from Philadelphia to Southend with a cargo of munitions, totalling more than 6,000 tons. While anchored in the Thames Estuary, the vessel drifted on to a sandbank while the captain slept, and broke its back. In the following days approximately half of the cargo was unloaded before the ship broke in two and sank. Ever since the salvage attempt was abandoned, *Richard Montgomery* has sat in the Thames Estuary in a strictly controlled exclusion zone, with half of its cargo of mixed munitions still in situ, and with growing concern at the likely risk and effects of an accidental or malicious detonation. The wreck is carefully monitored, and recent surveys have indicated cracks that could lead to the holds containing cluster munitions and other bombs being broken open, with a risk that this could cause an explosion. While debates about the stability of the cargo remain on-going, the likely impact of the detonation of the ship would be impressive: with a force equivalent to a small nuclear weapon, it would throw thousands of tons of water, sand and metal up to 10,000ft into the air, causing severe damage to the nearby town of Sheerness and sending a tidal wave up the Thames with potentially devastating effects. For this reason this wreck, with its masts protruding from the water adorned with warning signs, remains one of the most interesting and problematic archaeological sites in Britain's wartime heritage. Like all underwater wreck sites, the effects of tides, corrosion and shifting sands will eventually break up the ship; whether this can be pre-empted or controlled remains to be seen.

The Docks

Having survived the U–boats in the mid–Atlantic, the mines around the entrance to estuaries and the ever-present Luftwaffe threat, the convoys arrived in British ports to unload their cargoes and begin the return journey. In Liverpool, London, Bristol and other ports the infra-structure of the docks, including railways, cranes and warehouses, were just one more link in the chain that carried food, military supplies, oil and other essentials from their source to their end users. Like the ships that carried them, the ports that received these goods were subjected to relentless attacks by the German military machine. In many places the effects of these raids can still be seen in the areas around the ports, where few if any of the pre-war buildings survived the war. One of the most remarkable parts of the archaeology of Second World War Britain can be found not in Britain itself, but in the unlikely location of New York's East River Drive. There, a plaque was erected in 1942 marking the place where thousands of tons of rubble from the blitzed port city of Bristol was dumped to provide solid foundations. The plaque reads:

BRISTOL BASIN

BENEATH THIS EAST RIVER DRIVE OF THE CITY OF NEW YORK LIE STONES, BRICKS AND RUBBLE FROM THE BOMBED CITY OF BRISTOL IN ENGLAND . . . BROUGHT HERE IN BALLAST FROM OVERSEAS, THESE FRAGMENTS THAT ONCE WERE HOMES SHALL TESTIFY WHILE MEN LOVE FREEDOM TO THE RESOLUTION AND FORTITUDE OF THE PEOPLE OF BRITAIN. THEY SAW THEIR HOMES STRUCK DOWN WITHOUT WARNING . . . IT WAS NOT THEIR HOMES BUT THEIR VALOR THAT KEPT THEM FREE . . .

And broad-based under all
Is planted England's oaken-hearted mood,
As rich in fortitude
As e'er went worldward from the island–wall.

ERECTED BY THE ENGLISH-SPEAKING UNION OF THE UNITED STATES 1942

Many of the vessels that crossed the Atlantic arrived in Bristol to unload their cargoes. To return empty would have made them difficult to manoeuvre and potentially caused structural damage, so ballast was needed, and the blitzed buildings of Bristol provided an ideal solution, as the mounds of rubble themselves presented a logistical problem to the city. Once shipped back across the Atlantic, the rubble was used in various places, including along the waterfront in parts of New York, to provide solid foundations for construction on marshy land. Thus a small part of the archaeology of Second World War Britain became 'orphaned'.

In London the Thames Discovery Programme (TDP) has found numerous traces of the damage inflicted on the port by German bombs, as part of their wider survey into archaeological remains along the Thames foreshore. One of the most remarkable features that the TDP has recorded is the extensive damage to the river wall caused by bombing. While this might not sound particularly significant, in places the river wall is the only defence against catastrophic flooding of urban areas at particularly high tides, especially on the south side of the Thames. Research by the TDP found that special repair squads, the Thames Flood Unit, had been stationed along the river to effect immediate repairs to parts of the river wall at risk of flooding; some of the repairs were only a few metres wide, while others extended over a much larger area and required the dumping of tons of material to buttress the repairs. In several places along the river the effects of bombing on the docks can be clearly seen in the form of rubble and other remains still in place, especially where new structures have been built on top of them. At Billingsgate the bombed remains of the old iron wharf structure can be seen beneath the concrete wharf that replaced it. Along the Thames are the remains of hundreds of wrecked or broken vessels, their wooden ribs and metal plates poking out of the mud. The earliest are prehistoric, a few are medieval, but most date to the period from the industrial revolution to the present, including a number sunk by bombs during the Second World War. On the night of 29 December 1940 the Germans rained fire-bombs on the city, causing what was known as the Second Great Fire of London. The raid was timed to coincide with a very low tide on the Thames, so the fire-boats with their powerful pumps and monitors could not reach the fires and the fire brigade on land could not pump water from the river. A fire-fighter stationed on a Thames fire-boat described watching dozens of burning barges, broken free of their moorings, drift downriver towards the sea. No doubt many of these are among the anonymous wrecks that line the foreshore and periodically appear as the silt and mud are briefly scoured away by the tides.

The bomb-damage survey maps of London reveal how heavily the German bombers targeted the docks in the East End and all along the riverfronts in the Port of London. The Thames was a simple navigational aid for aircraft flying west from Germany, and the damage was immense: the vast nineteenth- and twentieth-century docks with their warehouses, cranes and other infrastructure were nearly annihilated in a series of raids in 1940–41, and the local populations suffered heavy casualties. Many of the residential areas around the docks were some of the poorest slums in London, and provision of air raid shelters in these places was generally utterly insufficient. The impact of bombing in these areas can be seen in what is not there any more: the pre-war houses and warehouses bombed to rubble. The 25,000 bombs that fell on the London docklands made them the most heavily hit non-military target in Britain in the Second World War.

Traces of War on, in and by the Waterfront

The transport of goods and resources from around the world into wartime Britain was a titanic effort by the largely civilian Merchant Navy. The traces that this long battle has left in the seas, on land and in the marginal areas in between is a remarkable material legacy that archaeologists will be exploring for years to come, and in this brief chapter I have only touched on some of the most iconic and recognisable remains such as the wreck of SS *James Eagan Lane*. It is worth mentioning in addition some of the other traces of the Second World War that line the inshore waters of the British Isles, the remarkable survivors of battles and campaigns from the outbreak of the war to its end.

In the run-up to D-Day, the invasion of Normandy by Allied forces in June 1944, a variety of new installations and structures were created in the areas around the south of England from where most of the invading forces sailed. In the 1990s English Heritage surveyed and recorded a number of the concrete slipways from which troops, supplies and vehicles were launched or loaded into landing craft and other vessels. Spread along the coast from Essex to Cornwall, many of these substantial sites have survived into the present, and some – such as the well preserved concrete slipways at Torquay – have become memorial sites where D-Day veterans gather to remember their comrades.

The Normandy landings of Operation Overlord used a number of remarkable technological innovations to achieve their ambitious aims, and traces of these can still be seen in sites around the British coast. To enable troops, vehicles and goods to be unloaded rapidly a harbour was needed, but no safe or accessible sites were available. Instead the Allies brought their own: the famous Mulberry Harbour built of prefabricated concrete sections that would be floated across the Channel and sunk or secured in place. The main sections of the Mulberry were rectangular concrete caissons weighing up to 6,000 tons each, which were towed across the Channel by tugs. While the remains of the Mulberry Harbours can still be seen on the landing beaches in Normandy, several of the caissons remained in Britain, and a number can still be seen today. After construction, most of the larger concrete components were sunk in shallow water to conceal them from German aerial photography, and were refloated shortly before deployment. Due to problems with the tugs, two of the caissons could not be refloated and remain submerged off Selsey Bill, forming an artificial reef popular with local divers for the number and variety of fish that congregate around them. In Portland Harbour two of the gigantic Phoenix caissons can still be seen towering out of the water, the last remainders of a group of ten brought back from Normandy after the war to form a breakwater. Like the wrecks of the Liberty Ships and U-boats, these and other traces of the Second World War are enduring reminders of the impact of the conflict on every part of the British landscape, including the seabed that surrounds it. Like SS *Richard Montgomery* and its dangerous cargo, the vast concrete blocks in Portland Harbour are impossible to ignore, their intrusive presence forcing an awareness of the war into the present.

Summary

By the end of the Second World War in Europe the Battle of the Atlantic had raged for almost six years, and millions of tons of shipping and cargo lay in wreckage on the seabed, along with thousands of seamen of all nations. The Battle of the Atlantic and the efforts of the Allied merchant navies to keep Britain supplied with food, fuel and war materials is one of the least well known stories of the Second World War. Unlike the Battle of Britain and the preparations for D-Day, most of this battlefront was fought at sea, out of sight of the population at large. As civilians, the merchant mariners enjoyed none of the benefits of paid leave, compensation for losses or medals that the armed forces received, even though they shared many of the same risks and suffered substantial losses. Today most of the archaeological traces of their struggle against the elements, as well as the German navy and air force, are hidden out of sight in the depths of the Atlantic or in the shallower but no-less-deadly inshore waters of Britain. The wrecks of the cargo vessels, tankers and other merchant ships that line our shores are slowly being broken up by the sea, and most are visible only to divers and fish. Only when they present a risk to shipping (or in the case of *Richard Montgomery*, to life and limb) do they come to anyone else's attention. However, as we have seen, there are still traces of the war at sea that can be found without donning scuba gear: the mine-watching stations at the entrances to harbours and estuaries around the country, the code-breaking site of Bletchley Park, and the bomb damage to the docks and waterfronts in London and other port cities around the country.

Further Reading

Bennett, G.H. and R. Bennett, *Survivors: British Merchant Seamen in the Second World War* (Hambledon, 2007)

Edwards, Bernard, *The Quiet Heroes: British Merchant Seamen at War* (Pen & Sword, 2002)

Elphick, Peter, *Life Line: the Merchant Navy at War* (Chatham, 1999)

Elphick, Peter, *Liberty: the Ships that Won the War* (Chatham, 2006)

Henry, Chris, *Depth Charge: Royal Navy Mines, Depth Charges and Underwater Weapons 1914–1945* (Leo Cooper, 2005)

Kurson, Robert, *Shadow Divers: the True Adventure of Two Americans Who Risked Everything to Solve One of the Last Mysteries of World War II* (Random House, 2004)

Lewis, William, *Under the Red Duster: the Merchant Navy in World War II* (Crowood, 2003)

Malcolm, Ian, *Life Aboard a Wartime Liberty Ship* (Amberley, 2010)

Milner, Marc, *Battle of the Atlantic* (History Press, 2011)

Preston, Anthony, *Jane's Fighting Ships of World War II* (Jane's, 1989)

Slader, John, *The Fourth Service: Merchantmen at War 1939–45* (Robert Hale, 1994)

Williams, Andrew, *The Battle of the Atlantic* (BBC Books, 2003)

Woodman, Richard, *The Real Cruel Sea: the Merchant Navy in the Battle of the Atlantic 1939–1943* (Pen & Sword, 2011)

Useful Websites

www.mna.org.uk and **www.red-duster.co.uk**

These are the websites for the Merchant Navy Association, with a wealth of information to explore including histories, forums and links.

www.convoyweb.org.uk

This site contains an incredible amount of information about the merchant ships and convoys of the Second World War.

Places to Visit

HMS *Belfast*

This museum ship is part of the Imperial War Museum and is moored on the Thames close to the Winston Churchill Britain at War Experience at London Bridge. A light cruiser commissioned in 1939, *Belfast* took part in D-Day and the hunt for *Scharnhorst*, as well as serving as a convoy escort. Today it is a museum ship dedicated to the history of the war at sea in the Second World War.

HMS *Belfast*
The Queen's Walk
London
SE1 2JH
www.iwm.org.uk/visits/hms-belfast

Western Approaches – Liverpool War Museum

This museum is housed in the heavily fortified former headquarters of Western Approaches Command, which coordinated much of the Battle of the Atlantic and many of the convoys that arrived in Britain during the Second World War. The building has been restored to its wartime state, with many original features including the map room where convoys and U-boat packs were charted.

Western Approaches – Liverpool War Museum
1–3 Rumford Street
Liverpool
L2 8SZ
www.liverpoolwarmuseum.co.uk/index.php

U-boat Story

The wreck of the German U-boat *U-534* was recovered from the bottom of the North Sea decades after being sunk by RAF aircraft in 1945. Today it is on display in Merseyside divided in four sections, containing exhibits and interactive displays about the history of the U-boat war.

U-Boat Story
Woodside Ferry Terminal
Mersey Ferries
Woodside
Birkenhead
Merseyside
CH41 6DU
www.u-boatstory.co.uk

Chapter 3

The War Child

For millions of children in Britain the outbreak of the Second World War in September 1939 coincided with the end of the long summer holiday and the start of the new school year. For many young people the subsequent delay before teaching began was a foretaste of the disruption that the war would bring into all aspects of their lives, from the food they ate and the clothes they wore to the terrors of bombing and the loss of homes, family members and friends. Six school years later the war ended, and the children of wartime Britain found themselves in an unfamiliar peacetime world. Many of the teenagers of 1939 were, by 1945, serving in the armed forces or in war work. For the younger children the world at war was the only one that they had ever known. The children of the Second World War experienced the conflict in the same way as most adults: its privations, dangers, excitements and fears. In turn, the world of total warfare intruded itself upon many aspects of children's lives, forcing air raid shelters onto their playing fields, mines onto their beaches, gas masks onto their shoulders and showering hot shrapnel out of the skies for them to play and trade with. The war turned buildings into bombsites and the children turned bombsites into playgrounds. This world of wartime childhood and the meagre traces that remain is the subject of this chapter.

For many young people in Britain the greatest immediate impact of the war was on their family life. Even before the outbreak of war many fathers had signed up in the armed forces and by September 1939 many were stationed abroad or away from home – a taste of things to come as the wars at sea, in North Africa and the Far East grew in prominence through the early years of the war. Alongside this widespread absence of fathers, there was a similar movement of mothers out of the home and into the workplace, although it would be wrong to suggest that mothers going to work was in any way unusual in this period. However, as more and more women began to work in industries to fill the gaps left by the call–up of men into the armed forces, many began to work away from home, and many children found themselves with an unusual degree of freedom. This erosion of the traditional family unit was regarded with suspicion in some official circles, and the fear of 'problem families' and feral children coloured many official views of British children in wartime – something that, in many cases, children took care to live up to.

The Second World War permeated every aspect of life in the combatant nations, and children's lives were not excluded. Many or most of these interventions were imposed by the adult world onto the children, such as the rationing of clothes, fuel and food (including, most outrageously, sweets). A more dramatic impact of the war was evacuation: tens of thousands of children were sent from their homes in towns and cities that were likely to be heavily bombed to stay with strangers in the countryside or in safer urban areas. The disruption of family life continued for those who were not evacuated, many of whom were forced by bombing to find new homes, or had bombed-out relatives and neighbours move in with them. For many in urban areas the disrupted sleep caused by night air raids led to families decamping to public shelters every evening, taking bedding and food and setting up camp in the noisy, smelly and often unhygienic basements, tunnels, underground stations and refuges.

The threat of air warfare meant that the population – children included – had to be prepared and trained in the use of protective equipment and installations. Not all of the militarisations of children's lives were so unwelcome: military themes in comics and films and other parts of popular culture spread into the creation of toys based on the latest aircraft, warships, tanks, weapons and uniforms, feeding a desire among many young people to get their hands on the 'real things'. Thus encouraged, many children integrated warlike themes into their play, re-enacting famous battles in streets and parks with toy weapons and home-made accoutrements. When they came across real artefacts of the war – bullets, shell fragments, incendiary bombs and the like – they collected and traded them avidly.

Of all the sites and artefacts associated with childhood in the Second World War, the two most iconic are probably the ubiquitous gas mask, carried at all times on pain of peril, and the school air raid shelter, where long hours were passed as German aircraft forced children and teachers out of their classrooms and into the comparative safety of reinforced basements or concrete rooms beneath playing fields. Another iconic image of the war years is that of children playing in the ruins of bombed buildings. The loss of many parks and beaches to the ever-hungry 'war effort' deprived children of many traditional play areas, and new ones were found in the pathetic broken heaps of bricks, tiles, wood and household goods that appeared with more and more frequency in neighbourhoods across the country as the bombing raids and V1 and V2 campaigns took their toll.

The 1939 school year was supposed to have seen the school leaving age raised to 15, but this was overruled by the outbreak of war, and many teenagers who had anticipated another year of schooling found themselves instead looking for work. This was just one of the negative effects that the war had on education: many young people who were evacuated lost out on schooling due to the disruption, and others were prevented from accessing further education due to the exigencies of wartime. The destruction or damage to schools in night bombing raids, while welcomed by most children at the time, also affected their access to learning. In later years many children of the Blitz came to regret and resent the educational and employment opportunities that they lost due to this disruption.

As the nation prepared for war it was natural that many young people would want to play a part in the activities taking place around them. Many boys found volunteer roles in Home Front organisations such as the Air Raid Warden Service and the Auxiliary Fire Service, acting as runners carrying messages between stations and crews, often in the midst of air raids. Similar roles were available to older boys in the Home Guard, often under the auspices of the Boy Scouts. A number of organisations such as the St John's Ambulance ran cadet schemes for older children, but the most popular were those run by the armed services: the Air Training Corps, the Sea Cadets and the Army Cadets. These were for boys only, but later organisations were established for girls to prepare for wartime service. There were numerous programmes promoted on the Home Front by the government that children took part in: collecting scrap metal, paper and other recyclables was a popular activity and one that sometimes brought a modest financial reward. Even more popular was small-scale agriculture in back gardens and allotments: 'digging for victory' by growing food to supplement rations, raising chickens for eggs, and rabbits and pigs for meat. Through all of these activities children could feel that they were 'doing their bit': a source of pride, and a psychologically important way of feeling involved in the nation's struggle.

The surge in ways to keep young people busy was in part driven by the fear of juvenile delinquency running riot in a country at war. With mothers at work, fathers at war, and extended family links broken by evacuation and the dispersal of bombed communities, there was an understandable fear that the social structure was at risk of fragmentation. One focus of popular concern was the public air raid shelter, feared as both a poorly ventilated pit of disease, and as a shadowy den of promiscuity, particularly for the young. While many young (and not so young) people did use public shelters as convenient spots for illicit assignations, a greater problem that was reported across the country was the vandalism of public shelters by children tearing out fittings and rendering the shelters unusable, to the extent that air raid wardens were instructed to padlock the shelters during the daytime. In the early years of the war there was a sharp rise in the number of children arrested and charged for crimes including vandalism and petty theft, although it is unclear to what extent this represents an actual increase in crime or merely a harsher policing of young people driven by a fear of juvenile delinquency and its wider social effects.

Some clues to the motives and means of unruly youths can be seen in the unusual case of the Battle of Barmouth in 1944, when three boys aged 12 to 14 stole rifles and bullets from the Royal Marines and forced an armed stand-off in the hills above the town. The boys involved felt that their town had been occupied twice-over: first by English-speaking evacuees, then by the Royal Marines, and that amidst all the excitement, as Barmouth was transformed into a military camp in preparation for D-Day, they were isolated and bored. Security within the town was lax, and the boys had already tried to steal a light machine gun before their successful attempt on the Marines' armoury, where they took three small-calibre rifles and several thousand rounds of ammunition through a back-window. Having made good their escape, the boys retreated into the hills above the town and set about firing off most of the ammunition at nothing in particular, apart from a few hens. The theft was discovered and the boys were pursued by police, but they retreated under fire, and successively large troops of Marines attempted to storm the boys' hideout in a disused mine, firing blank ammunition. The stand-off lasted for several days before the boys, having fired off almost all of the ammunition, surrendered and were marched into the town under arrest. No one had been harmed in the escapade, and Churchill's demand that the boys be tried for attempted murder went unheeded – after a short time in a Borstal they were released. The boys' resentment at the encroachment of the war into their lives was combined with a fascination with all things military and a large dose of boredom – a common enough combination in wartime Britain, albeit with a decidedly uncommon outcome.

Children's exposure to the realities of total war came with the obvious corollary that children would be among the tens of thousands of British civilians killed and injured in the Second World War. Despite evacuation, ARP training and the provision of air raid shelters, many thousands of children died in bombing in London and other towns and cities across the country. In 1943 the Luftwaffe conducted nuisance raids on London, with small groups of fighter-bomber aircraft flying at low altitude and high speed to avoid detection, and bombing and strafing targets on the ground. One such attack targeted a school in Catford, South London, apparently deliberately. Thirty-eight children were killed alongside six teachers, and many more were injured. In total, around 7,700 children under 16 were killed by enemy action in Britain during the Second World War, and a similar number injured. Alongside these tragic figures is the unknown number of children who suffered severe psychological damage as a result of air raids and other factors: rates of Post-Traumatic Stress Disorder (PTSD) among these children of the Blitz was found to be extraordinarily high.

It would be wrong to suggest that there is a single story of wartime childhood. In fact there was a vast variety of experiences based on differences of geography, age, class and gender. Children living in urban areas were generally much more exposed to bombing and other aspects of warfare than children in rural areas, while those living in industrial or port cities were particularly hard-hit. For those children who were evacuated to rural areas the disconnection from family and community created a distinctive war experience; even stronger in the thousands of children evacuated to America, Canada and other safer overseas destinations. For older children gender differences came into play as boys were more likely to serve as volunteers for ARP, fire and rescue services.

Socio-economic class played a significant part, particularly in access to education, good food and luxuries such as comics amidst the privations of war. Perhaps the most important determinant of war experience for children was age: a child born in 1929 might have begun the war in junior school and ended it working in a war-related industry; a child born in 1939 would have ended the war in infant school having known no other world than the one at war. The principal focus of this chapter is the majority of children in wartime Britain who lived in towns or cities but were not evacuated, and who were old enough to remember the world before the bombs began to fall.

Where is the archaeology and heritage of the children of Second World War Britain? Much of it lies buried beneath school playing fields and in rubble beneath the rebuilt post-war cities. Much more of it lies at the back of cupboards and drawers, in attics and in old suitcases. These stray artefacts – gas masks, ration books, badges, shrapnel fragments and other souvenirs of war – are as much part of the archaeological heritage of wartime as the bunkers that dot the countryside and the wrecks of the deep Atlantic. Together they contribute small chapters to the story of life in Second World War Britain. The children of the Blitz will soon be the only ones left to tell the story of the war, and after them we will have only their artefacts, their places and the stories they have told.

Schools in Wartime

While school looms large in any child's life, in the Second World War schools took on a number of additional roles in preparing children for life in wartime. Schools served a number of purposes in the war – both as communities of adults and children, and as buildings. A large number of schools suffered damage or destruction in bombing or in V1 and V2 attacks later in the war, and many former children of the Blitz recall the delight at finding their school bombed. Alongside bomb damage many schools found some or all of their buildings requisitioned by the government for use as auxiliary fire stations, ambulance stations, air raid warden posts or command centres, bases for rescue squads and a range of other uses. These new uses often involved adaptations to the buildings and the loss of playing fields as well.

At the outbreak of war many schools stayed closed until they could provide adequate air raid shelter protection for staff and students. This caused a number of practical and political problems: as the country geared up for war, there was a shortage of the materials and components for air raid shelters such as concrete, steel sheet and reinforcing bars. In many places schools were low on the list of priorities for such materials, and local education authorities quibbled about whether they or central government should pick up the hefty bill for this nationwide programme of construction. Some school shelters were built as individual structures on or under playing fields, while some took the form of structural reinforcements to existing basement rooms or corridors. As shelters were completed, many schools began to reopen gradually, class by class. Up until this point many classes had been meeting on an ad hoc basis in pupils' homes, church halls and other available buildings, with many schools running classes in morning and afternoon shifts.

The evacuation of children from certain target areas to rural areas was coordinated through schools, and children were evacuated in school groups (although they were individually housed at their destinations). This meant that children were accompanied on these often traumatic journeys by their friends and familiar teachers. For some time after the outbreak of war there was little or no bombing in most cities and many parents retrieved their children from evacuation areas – many returning home shortly before the outbreak of the Blitz in the autumn of 1940. In 1944 there was a renewed push to evacuate children from London in response to the V1 and later the V2 rocket attacks.

Schools also played an important role in educating students about air raid precautions and civil defence in general. While gas masks had been distributed to most of the population from 1938 onwards, it was in schools that children were taught how to quickly don their mask in response to warning signals, and teachers were trained to check that masks were properly fitted and worn. Gas mask drills in schools consisted of students quickly putting on their masks and then continuing with their regular school activities, including lessons, gymnastics and play. Schools were the only place where carrying gas masks was compulsory, and students who forgot their masks were sent home to pick them up. Schools were also used in live gas tests, discussed in more detail below. Alongside gas drills there were regular air raid drills. On hearing a whistle or siren the children were trained to file out of their classroom (walking, not running) and to march into the shelters, taking their seats on the benches. Some shelters were plain concrete bunkers with meagre lighting, and children passed the time during actual air raids by singing songs or chanting their times tables. Better equipped shelters had proper lighting and air conditioning, and in these shelters lessons could continue without a break. Some schools encouraged students to decorate the interiors of the shelters with murals and other designs to make them more welcoming and less grim.

Excavating a School Air Raid Shelter

In 2005 students at Edgware Junior School in north London discovered a strip of concrete sticking out of the ground at the edge of their playing field. The school had been aware of air raid shelters somewhere in its grounds but the precise locations had remained a mystery, so the school invited a local archaeological society to investigate. In early 2006 we began to examine the site: by this time some of the children, curious about the site, had cleared more earth from the concrete structure which appeared to be the outline of an entrance staircase, lying level with the ground. On the flat surface of the playing field no shelters could be seen, apart from a few very slight raised areas, barely 5cm higher than the surrounding ground.

Before starting to excavate we carried out a geophysical survey of the playing field, using variations in the conductivity of the soil to trace subterranean structures. This survey revealed the presence of several more structures, aside from the one we were investigating: up to eight in total. Government regulations restricted the size of school shelters, so that no more than fifty children could be in any one shelter: there were fears that a direct hit on a communal school shelter might wipe out an entire school. Following these guidelines, all of the shelters at Edgware School appeared from this survey to have been spaced several metres apart.

A study of documents in the Barnet Local Studies & Archive Centre revealed more of the history of the shelters, of which there were originally (allegedly) thirteen constructed in 1939–40. Like many schools in London, Edgware School had remained closed until the shelters were constructed, several months into the school year. During this time classes were taught in a nearby hall and in students' homes. The shelters were built by a local construction firm, Lavender Macmillan

Ltd, for a cost of £258 10s each. No documents from this firm had survived so it was impossible to tell exactly where the shelters had been put in, what form they had taken or even what they were built from, as Lavender Macmillan reportedly installed both steel and concrete shelters, depending on cost and availability of materials. It appears that the shelters built at Edgware School were the more expensive, safer and longer-lasting concrete versions.

Records revealed that the shelters had been upgraded several times in the years after their installation, with lighting, heating and ventilation installed at various points. They also revealed, crucially, that in 1945 they had been stripped of their fittings and sealed up with concrete. This seemed to indicate a tougher excavation than we had anticipated! Armed with a sledgehammer and a giant crowbar, we set about excavating the entrance staircase of the first shelter that we had identified.

The first task was to clear the earth out of the staircase, a dirty and slippery job that proceeded quickly, as step after step of the original concrete stairs were uncovered and cleaned. Mixed in with the mud were big chunks of the concrete we had feared would seal the site completely, none of them bigger than a paving slab. At the same time we began digging a smaller trench to reveal the top of the roof of the shelter so that we could better assess the construction methods and see how deep it had been buried. Towards the bottom of the staircase we found a large free-standing gas lamp/heater buried in the soil; presumably it was part of the backup for the shelter in case the electricity cut out. Once the staircase was clear, we were able to step inside the shelter, shine our torches into the darkness and see what we had uncovered. Meanwhile the excavation of the shelter roof hit concrete at a depth of around 45cm, and found that the roof of the shelter had been painted with tar to make it more water-resistant.

The walls and ceiling of the shelter, as seen from the inside, were constructed from concrete slabs 45 centimetres wide and 2 metres high. The floor was poured concrete with a drainage sump at the bottom of the stairs. It was approximately 16 metres long and 2 metres wide (about the size of a small train carriage), with two brick toilet cubicles, one at each end – fortunately the chemical toilets had already been removed. At the end furthest from the staircase was a steel ladder leading up to an emergency escape hatch that emerged, we discovered, in the middle of the playing field. Having completed our measurements, we started looking for signs of habitation. At the bottom of the escape ladder was a big pile of refuse which we began to sort through: it appeared to be school rubbish dating to roughly 1945 that had been thrown down to dispose of it shortly before the shelter was sealed. This rubbish heap included parts of a car engine, glass bottles and jars, rusted tin cans, a pair of shoes, and various toys and oddments including a toy jeep and assorted marbles. Some of the glass jars had dried paint inside them, suggesting that they had been collected by the school for use in art classes. These artefacts brought the inhabitants of the shelter to life as school children painting and playing in the midst of a war.

We surveyed the walls of the shelter systematically looking for graffiti or names written on the concrete. We found only one – a drawing of a sailing ship in yellow chalk. However, one of the toilet cubicle walls – facing the length of the shelter – was covered in long division sums, without the answers written in. Presumably lessons carried on in the shelter during air raids, and the class had been in the midst of a maths lesson when the all-clear sounded for one of the last air raids of the war and they returned to their desks, not realising that the chalk marks on the brickwork would still be there, as fresh as the day they were written, more than sixty years later.

Before the dig we had tried to trace former students who had attended Edgware School during the war years, so that we could interview them about their experiences and invite them to revisit the shelter. By the time the dig began we had traced one former student who agreed to visit the excavation. Mrs Smith turned out to have a wealth of memories of the school in wartime, as well as the local area, and she was generous enough with her time to field questions from the archaeologists and from the 10- and 11-year-old school students. For us it was fascinating to have a living witness to our archaeological site, and Mrs Smith's memories of using the shelters chimed with many of our findings, including the cramped seating and the damp, musty underground smell. Many of her stories added life to our picture of the shelters: she sang some of the songs that students used to pass the time, showed us how gas-mask drills were conducted, and explained how children had collected pieces of shell shrapnel to trade in the schoolyard. We discovered that the chemical toilets were only ever used in extreme circumstances as no one wanted to pee where everyone else could hear them. In addition to these illuminating stories, she also resolved one of the questions that had been troubling us: where were the other shelters? Our survey had counted around eight on the playing field, but the records stated that there had been thirteen. Mrs Smith showed us where the shelters for the infants' school had been – in an area that is now under tarmac.

The shelters were not the only traces of the Second World War at Edgware School. On one of the walls was a faded painted sign that read WATCH ROOM. The school logbook recorded that part of the school building had been given over to the Auxiliary Fire Service, and that they had cut a hole in one of the walls to drive their fire appliance in and out. This section of wall with a later brick repair can still be seen, as well as hooks inside the building where the hoses were hung to dry. Documents in the local archive showed that at the end of the war the fire service paid the school several hundred pounds' compensation for damage to the playing field and other facilities.

The Edgware School air raid shelter project shows how archaeology, history and memory can come together to shed light on a near-forgotten piece of Second World War heritage. Not only did this combination of sources benefit us, the researchers, but it also provided the school students with a chance to learn about history outside the classroom. Hearing about the past from an eyewitness and seeing objects brought to the surface (including some old children's toys) made it a very unusual history lesson.

Gas Masks

In photographs and film footage from Second World War Britain it is often difficult to know that there was a war on. People go about their everyday lives and children play in clothes that could date from the 1930s to 1950s. What often marks a photograph out as a wartime image are the small rectangular boxes that many of the people are wearing, hung on strings over their shoulders: gas mask cases for the ubiquitous General Civilian Respirator. More than forty million of these masks were distributed to the public before and during the war. Many remain in private ownership, many more are owned or displayed by museums around the country, and they are often found in junk shops or for sale online. Many still have the name and address of their original owners written inside the box, so that a lost mask (identical to millions of others!) could be reunited with its owner. For children in the Second World War the gas mask was an ever-present reminder of the war and often an unwelcome one. The uses and abuses that children found for their gas masks were practical, inventive and anarchic: the life story of this one artefact can tell us a great deal about children's lives in Second World War Britain.

It is difficult to imagine the widespread terror of gas warfare in 1930s culture. The memory of chlorine and phosgene gas in the First World War was still fresh, and there were tens of thousands of wheezing gas casualties as living reminders of the horrors of poison gas. In 1930s science fiction and in military planning the spectre of gas bombing took on an apocalyptic tone similar to the fear of nuclear attack during parts of the Cold War. There were sceptical views as well: the scientist J.B.S. Haldane, who helped develop gas masks in the First World War, believed that dropping gas on cities would be relatively pointless – if people stayed indoors and closed their windows the gas would be rapidly dispersed by the wind. Observing the bombing of Barcelona in the Spanish Civil War, Haldane came to the conclusion that high explosive bombs and incendiary bombs were much more efficient weapons and posed a much greater threat to British cities. In a sense the gas mask was a political compromise to the public's fear of air attack: while large, deep-buried municipal air raid shelters could have provided much more effective protection to the public from all kinds of attack, the General Civilian Respirator at 2 shillings a-piece was a much cheaper proposition. In the event poison gas was not used in bombing civilian populations, in part due to fear of reprisals and in part due to its lack of effectiveness. A ton of explosives could and did do a lot more damage to a nation's war effort than a ton of poison gas.

The need for gas protection in a future war had been recognised by the Home Office as early as 1924, but it was not until ten years later that it became clear that, in the event of war, the population would demand access to cheap gas masks. The government's Chemical Research Committee began work on a cheap mask in 1934, with a view to selling them to the public, but following the use of poison gas by the Italian military in Abyssinia in 1935 mass production was ordered on the understanding that masks would be distributed free of charge. In 1936 a disused cotton mill in Blackburn was transformed into a gas mask factory, with the aim of producing forty million masks within two years.

The General Civilian Respirator consisted of several parts: a rubber face-piece with a cellulose window; a metal tin containing the filtering materials (mostly charcoal); and a mass of cotton webbing to hold it on the face, secured with clips, slides and safety pins. The masks came in several sizes, the smallest designed for use by children aged 5 and over. This raised a serious problem: until as late as 1938 no thought had been given to gas protection for children under 5, and only a little work had been carried out on gas protection for babies. When gas masks for adults and older children were first distributed in 1938 many parents refused to take them, arguing that they did not want protection from gas if their children were left unprotected. In response to this demand, a smaller gas mask was developed for young children – the so-called 'Mickey Mouse' mask made of red rubber with a brightly painted filter capsule to make it resemble a toy. Parents were encouraged to wear their gas mask in front of their children and to make a game of it, so that in the event of gas attacks the children would not be frightened of the sight of their parents in black rubber masks. For babies the 'baby bag' was introduced, a novel type of protection which fitted over the entire upper half of the body and was kept supplied with air from a pump.

Schools made it compulsory for students to carry gas masks, although it was never a legal requirement for adults, and the proportion of the population carrying masks fluctuated between around 10 and 75 per cent. In schools children carried out gas mask drills, as well as rather brutal 'live gas tests' in which they were immersed in tear gas to check that the masks were functioning and properly fitted. For these tests mobile gas chambers were assembled in schoolyards and children wearing gas masks were forced to sit in clouds of teargas, breathing hard, so that broken or ill-fitting masks could be detected. Some of the gas chamber operators, in violation of the strict rules, would pull children's masks off to expose them to the corrosive gas. Their intention was to impress upon the children the importance of carrying their gas masks at all times, and no doubt they were successful, but it seems a rather brutal form of teaching.

In children's hands the gas masks soon took on a range of other uses. Swinging the masks on their strings became a version of giant conkers, and the flimsy cardboard cases soon disintegrated under this boisterous treatment, and in their not uncommon use as footballs. Other uses for gas masks included scaring younger siblings, making rude noises and (closer to their intended uses) using outside privies. Some children of the Blitz recall disguising themselves with gas masks for a variety of petty crimes and elaborate war games. The cardboard cases were soon superseded by a range of alternatives, as shops such as Woolworths spotted a market in metal cases, and parents created hand-made cases of cloth or patent leather. Photographs from the early years of the war often show this diversity of cases, which also served as handbags and hiding places for treasures. When, at the end of the war, there was a half-hearted effort to collect masks from the population, some of the cases were found to contain such oddments as mouldy sandwiches, false teeth, marbles and sweets.

The gas mask was the artefact that most clearly represents the popular experience of the Second World War, particularly for children. Many former children of the Blitz can still recall the rubber smell, blurred vision and the sticky, claustrophobic feeling of their gas mask, whether the Mickey Mouse version for younger children or the General Civilian Respirator for older children. Even those (and they were many) who ceremonially burnt their gas masks on the VE Day bonfires can still remember the ever-present box knocking against them as they ran, walked or cycled around.

Collections

Children in all places and in all periods have enjoyed collecting and swapping things, whether cigarette cards, marbles, football stickers or toy cars. During the Second World War this collecting and trading was one of the principal means by which the archaeology of the war became the archaeology of childhood in war, as children of the Blitz integrated all kinds of war materials into their games. Memories and diaries of the war years suggest that collecting bullets, badges, buttons, shrapnel and other artefacts of war was a common experience for children of all ages, from under-5s to teenagers, and among both boys and girls.

The war materials that children collected varied considerably. Some collected military cap badges and buttons donated by fathers or older brothers in the forces, although these were also often given by servicemen to their girlfriends as keepsakes. Bullets and cartridge cases were also sought after, as were larger objects taken from military training sites such as grenade pins and fragments, mortar bomb tail-fins and the nose cones of shells. However, the most common source of military collectibles for children in the Blitz were the artefacts that literally fell out of the sky like ripe conkers. These included fragments of bombs, the steel tail-fins of incendiary bombs, pieces of shot-down aircraft, bullets and bullet cases from air-to-air dogfights, and the most common category – shrapnel.

Anti-aircraft guns fired 3.7- or 4.5-inch shells at the rate of up to twenty per minute. The shells exploded at pre-determined altitudes, and the shell fragments – red-hot pieces of broken mild steel – ripped into enemy aircraft. In practice, almost 2,000 shells were fired on average for each German bomber destroyed, and many of the shells failed to explode, falling to earth as dangerous unexploded munitions, often in built-up areas. The shell fragments fell from the sky and landed like hot metal hail on rooftops and in streets, striking sparks from pavements and cobbles as they hit. Air raid wardens, firefighters and others outside during air raids wore steel helmets not to protect them against bombs or bullets but against shrapnel, which in the First World War killed almost as many as the German bombers did.

The morning after an air raid children of all ages would be out in the streets hoovering up every stray fragment of shrapnel, and huddling in playgrounds to compare their treasures, and to trade the finest pieces among them. Most of the shells were made of steel, which tore into jagged irregular fragments in the explosion, falling in pieces of all sizes, some as small as gravel and some as much as 12 inches long. Larger pieces were inevitably worth more than smaller, but in addition any fragment with text on it – a maker's mark or serial number – was worth substantially more. Even more 'valuable' were the nose cones of the shells, which had brass fuse rings around them. Fragments of these rings with their numerical scales were worth more than any steel fragment, and a complete nose-cone was a treasure nearly beyond price, which could be exchanged for any number of smaller pieces of shrapnel or for other rarities such as American comics. The trade and exchange of shrapnel and other wartime collectibles was conducted with great seriousness and ceremony.

Shrapnel collections could also find a use in the war effort. In some places children were encouraged to hand over their finds in scrap metal drives, to be recycled into new shells. Some children held exhibitions of their collections to raise money for war bonds. In most cases the shrapnel and other artefacts were held too dear to be handed over to scrap collectors, and the economy of the playground prevailed. Shrapnel could be traded for cigarette cards, sweets and other desirable commodities that young children treasure. Pieces of shell rust quickly, and most shrapnel collections were thrown away after the war. A few survive in museum collections and in private hands, while some prize pieces have been retained as paperweights or mementos. It is interesting to note that collecting military artefacts during wars is a very common practice for children around the world. German children in the Second World War were also collecting shell and bomb fragments, while children in Lebanon, the former Yugoslavia, Israel and other war zones around the world have found that collecting bullets, rocket fragments and other militaria is a way of coping with war trauma and retaining a sense of control in a scary world.

Bombsites

Deprived of many of their parks and beaches, and often discouraged from playing in school playgrounds, the children of Second World War Britain had few places to call their own. The places they found were bombsites: the ruins of houses and other buildings destroyed by bombs. These suited the children's needs perfectly: bombsites were dangerous, curious, forbidden spaces for climbing, building, hiding and a whole assortment of games. Many endured in British towns and cities into the 1950s and 1960s, and generations of post-war children found the same pleasures in rampaging through ruins. The children's book *The Otterbury Incident* describes the attraction of these ruins to imaginative children: the 'Incident' is the name of a bombsite where a group of boys play war-games, 'just the right sort of place – a mass of rubble, pipes, rafters, old junk, etc.'.

A house hit by a bomb would be reported by an air raid warden and fire crews, ambulance and rescue crews would attempt to extinguish any fires and extricate the residents from the ruins or from their shelter. The rescue crews would attempt to seal off leaking gas or water pipes, and rubble that had fallen into the street would be piled back onto the ruin. If only bodies or body-parts could be retrieved, these would be removed by the ambulance crews. If the residents had survived the bombing then they might try to rescue valuables or undamaged furniture from the house to save them from looters. With a tape or string barricading it off,

Plate 1: Traces of war: the burnt-out remains of Christ Church Greyfriars in the City of London, destroyed in the Blitz on 29 December 1940.

Plate 2: An unusual elevated pillbox located next to the railway line south of Putney Bridge station, South London.

Plate 3: Archaeologists carrying out a resistivity survey, looking for underground air raid shelters.

Plate 4: Recording part of an underground air raid shelter uncovered by excavation in London.

Plate 5: Recording an oral history interview on a Second World War excavation.

Plate 6: Excavating bombed houses in East London, with (*inset*), a fork found in the remains of a bombed house.

Plate 7: Excavating a Second World War site at Shooters Hill, South London.

Plate 8: Interviewing a veteran of the Home Guard at an excavation in Shooters Hill, South London.

Plate 9: Surviving pillbox near Shalford, Surrey.

Plate 10: Modern reconstruction of a spigot mortar position in Elvetham Heath, Hampshire.

Plate 11: Octagonal pillbox in Winchfield, Hampshire.

Plate 12: Excavated remains of a slit trench in Eaglesfield Park, Shooters Hill, South London.

Plate 13: Spigot mortar emplacement outside the Muckleburgh Military Collection in Weybourne, Norfolk.

Plate 14: The remains of bomb damage on the Thames at Billingsgate wharf.

Plate 15: Second World War coastal defences inside Plymouth harbour.

Plate 16: A mine-watcher's post at Tripcock Ness, with the remains of unusual plastic armour.

Plate 17: The wreck of the SS *Richard Montgomery* as it appears today, surrounded by warning signs.

Plate 18: A toy aircraft found during the excavation of a bombsite in East London.

Plate 19: Chalk drawing of a sailing boat found on the wall of an air raid shelter at Edgware School.

Plate 20: The entrance to the air raid shelter at Edgware School prior to excavation.

Plate 21: Painted sign on the wall of Edgware School hinting at its wartime use as an auxiliary fire station.

Plate 22: Excavating the buried entrance to the air raid shelter at Edgware School.

Plate 23: The interior of the air raid shelter at Edgware School, with (*inset*), a toy jeep that was found inside the shelter.

Plate 24: David Murray with some of the thousands of military and prisoner of war artefacts he recovered from the Wynches Camp site.

Plate 25: Aviation archaeologists recovering the engine block of Ray Holmes' Hurricane.

Plate 26: The control column of Ray Holmes' Hurricane, recovered from the ground after seventy years, encrusted in dirt and corrosion.

Plate 27: Fragments of a manufacturer's plate from Ray Holmes' Hurricane.

Plate 28: The remains of the airfield control tower at RAF Ludham.

Plate 29: Second World War B1 Hangar at RAF Grimsby, one of several wartime buildings surviving on the site that have been reused for various purposes.

Plate 30: An emergency exit shaft for an air raid shelter in Sunny Hill Park, Hendon.

Plate 31: The excavated entrance to an air raid shelter in Sunny Hill Park, Hendon.

Plate 32: Wiring for electricity in an air raid shelter in Sunny Hill Park, Hendon.

Plate 33: The emergency exit shaft of an air raid shelter in Sunny Hill Park, Hendon.

Plate 34: Removing the concrete cap from the emergency exit shaft of an air raid shelter in Sunny Hill Park, Hendon.

Plate 35: The emergency exit shaft for an air raid shelter in Sunny Hill Park, Hendon, with the original steel cover replaced.

Plate 36: Remains of a private air raid shelter in a garden in Edgware, North London.

Plate 37: Original air raid shelter sign found during the excavation at Sunny Hill Park, Hendon.

Plate 38: Interior view of a sealed-up staircase of an air raid shelter in Sunny Hill Park, Hendon.

the ruin would be left until needed as a site for a temporary water tank or some other purpose: many were simply left empty. Once the emergency services and any bystanders had drifted away, the site was abandoned until such time as weeds, wild animals and the local children began to colonise it.

The death, destruction, disruption and change wrought by bombing caused serious traumatic effects in many children of the Blitz. In studies conducted during and after the war by child psychologists such as Anna Freud, children who experienced air raids were found to have similar levels of post-traumatic stress disorder to soldiers who had experienced front-line combat. These studies showed that children were more affected if the adults around them appeared frightened, or if they experienced bombing while separated from parents and other familiar adults. In keeping with the idea that children 'master' the world around them through the games that they play, it might well have been the case that playing with shrapnel, kicking gas masks around and turning bombsites into playgrounds was a way for children in Second World War Britain to cope with the intrusion of the war into their lives and the changes it brought to the world around them.

In most cities bombsites were forbidden spaces, with access restricted to prevent looting and to prevent people being injured by falling brickwork or collapsing floors. In practice, it was impossible to prevent children from colonising these spaces and turning them into playgrounds. Some of the most common games played on bombsites were, unsurprisingly, war-games, with children taking on the roles of British and German troops battling with toy guns amidst the piles of rubble and broken walls: it was traditional that the German side should lose. There are also many accounts of children playing more domestic games in the bombsites: carefully piling up bricks and rafters to make tiny homes or rooms and 'playing house' with the remnants of household goods found in the ruins. For many children the bombsites were simply places to explore, climbing up broken staircases and shinning up drainpipes, risking life and limb to climb onto sagging roofs and half-collapsed floors. Mostly their aim was simply to explore, but some indulged in salvage (or more properly looting), dragging useful objects from the rubble. Some recall dragging broken or rusty prams and bicycles out of bombsites to build into go-carts, while there are accounts of children retrieving gas meters filled with half-pennies – a proper treasure chest.

Given the inherent dangers of bombsites it in unsurprising that some children were killed or seriously injured while playing on them, often by falls or by being hit by falling bricks and tiles.

As time passed, many bombsites were colonised by purple willow weed, a tenacious and hardy plant that became known colloquially as 'bombsite' or 'fire-weed'. Pools of water on bombsites became natural ponds and homes for all sorts of insect life. In many inner cities bombsites became the only natural, wild spaces around – and wild children were part of this ecology. The same child psychologists who monitored war trauma noticed the pleasure that children took in bombsite games, and in the post-war era they encouraged the creation of 'adventure playgrounds'. These rather rough-looking spaces lacked traditional playground equipment of slides and swings: instead they had piles of bricks, tyres, planks and wooden crates to build and rebuild dens and structures of their own design. These playgrounds replaced the bombsites that were being redeveloped and rebuilt in city centres and elsewhere, until by the 1970s most had disappeared. In 2005 the Museum of London excavated a bombsite in East London as a community heritage project, digging through the rubble to reveal the foundations of the houses underneath. Among the local people who gathered to watch the excavation were many who had grown up in the area during the war years, and among the stories they told – some of them hilariously naughty and marginally criminal – were tales of playing, fighting, hiding, hoarding and gallivanting amidst the ruined houses. The few bombsites that survive and the thousands that lie buried under parks and modern buildings bear witness to the terrors and small pleasures of wartime childhood.

The rush to prepare Britain for war meant that children's needs and interests were often pushed to the background; the lack of gas masks for children and the late rush of shelter building in schools shows how even providing protection to children was in many cases an afterthought for official planners. Despite this official indifference, the children of wartime Britain found their own ways of fighting and surviving the war. Collecting shrapnel and other war materials was therapeutic and fun, while kicking gas masks around like footballs and vandalising air raid shelters showed their annoyance and frustration at the restrictions that the war imposed on their lives. Amidst the destruction, chaos and dangers of the Home Front many children found consolation in playing amidst the wild ruins and claiming bombsites as children's places. Many of the traces of wartime childhood have been lost – bombsites buried, air raid shelters sealed up and forgotten, shrapnel collections and gas masks thrown away. At the same time some of these sites and artefacts remain: bombsites are just a few inches below the grass in many urban parks, schools show the scars and traces of wartime uses, and many old cupboards and wardrobes contain gas masks, ATC badges and other souvenirs with stories attached to them.

Further Reading

Brown, Mike, *Evacuees: Evacuation in Wartime Britain 1939–1945* (History Press, 2005)

Brown, Mike, *Evacuees of the Second World War* (Shire, 2009)

Brown, Mike, *Wartime Childhood* (Shire, 2009)

Brown, Mike, *A Child's War: Growing up on the Home Front* (History Press, 2010)

Gardiner, Juliet, *Wartime: Britain 1939–1945* (Headline, 2004)

Gardiner, Juliet, *The Children's War: The Second World War Through the Eyes of the Children of Britain* (Portrait, 2005)

Harrisson, Tom, *Living Through the Blitz* (Faber & Faber, 2010)

Levine, Joshua, *Forgotten Voices of the Blitz and the Battle of Britain* (Ebury Press, 2006)

Smith, Lyn, *Young Voices: British Children Remember the Second World War* (Viking, 2007)

Summers, Julie, *When the Children Came Home: Stories of Wartime Evacuees* (Simon & Schuster, 2011)

Werner, Emmy, *Through the Eyes of Innocents: Children Witness World War II* (Westview, 2000)

Westall, Robert, *Children of the Blitz: Memories of Wartime Childhood* (Macmillan, 1995)

Useful Websites

www.homesweethomefront.co.uk

An interesting collection of historical snippets from the Home Front, including sections on rationing, evacuation and air raid shelters.

www.bbc.co.uk/history/ww2peopleswar/
The BBC People's War website contains tens of thousands of stories by people who lived through the war, including those who fought and those on the Home Front. It is the most extraordinary archive of wartime memories and a unique resource for learning about the history of the Second World War.

Places to Visit

Winston Churchill's Britain at War Experience

This atmospheric theme museum close to London Bridge station aims to bring the world of Second World War Britain to life. It is principally aimed at school groups, with educational activities and dressing-up clothes.

64–66 Tooley Street
London Bridge
London SE1 2TF
www.britainatwar.co.uk

Chapter 4

The Prisoner of War

In March 1940 there were 257 German prisoners of war (PoWs) in Britain – by the end of the war this number had grown more than a thousand-fold, and prisoner of war camps had sprung up on farmland and open spaces around the country. In 1948 the last German PoWs returned home, having been kept as cheap labour in the rebuilding of Britain's towns and rural economy. As quickly as they had grown up, the PoW camps faded away: tents and temporary buildings were demolished and fences taken down, and new urban developments soon covered many of the hundreds of camp sites. Over the years traces of the prisoners of war and their presence in Britain have come to light: old hidden escape tunnels have been discovered; rubbish pits have offered a glimpse into everyday life in PoW camps; and in a few places parts of the camps have survived as farm buildings, heritage sites or industrial estates. The archaeology of German PoWs is revealing more and more about the hundreds of thousands of men who passed through the camps and the tens of thousands who stayed to make their homes in Britain. The artefacts, artworks and secrets that they left behind can help to reveal the human faces of the men who, for a while at least, were the only glimpse of the 'enemy' that most people in Britain ever saw.

Franz von Werra

On 5 September 1940 Leutnant Franz von Werra crash-landed his Messerschmitt 109 into a field in Kent and became a prisoner of war. By April 1941 he was back in Germany: the only German PoW to make a successful escape from Allied custody in the Second World War. Famous today as 'The One that Got Away', the account of von Werra's captivity serves to illuminate the common experience of thousands of German PoWs in Allied hands. His numerous escape attempts have gone down in history, and in one case at least – the escape tunnel dug by

'Swanwick Excavations Inc.' – there are archaeological traces of his colourful career in captivity.

Franz von Werra was born in 1914 in Leuk, Switzerland, and was raised by foster-parents, joining the Luftwaffe in 1936. In 1940, as Adjutant of II Gruppe, Jagdgeschwader 3, he took part in the French campaign. In May 1940 he was credited with destroying an RAF Hurricane and two French Breguet bombers. In August 1940 he controversially claimed to have shot down nine Hurricanes in a raid over Britain; he was eventually credited with four kills.

On 5 September 1940 von Werra's flight served as bomber escorts in a raid on south London. During the attack the German force was intercepted by Spitfires, and von Werra's plane sustained engine damage, forcing him to crash-land in a field at Loves Farm near Marden, Kent. Von Werra was unhurt in the crash and, after destroying some paperwork that he was carrying with him, he was taken captive by an anti-aircraft unit – specifically, by its cook. Thus he entered into the chain of custody that characterised the PoW experience at this early stage of the war, part of the first thousand of what was ultimately more than 400,000 German troops who would spend time in captivity in Britain.

After a night in the local police cells, von Werra was taken to Maidstone Barracks, before being transferred to the London District Cage for PoWs in Kensington Palace Gardens. Here he faced his first interrogation: a disarmingly friendly chat with a German-speaking British officer. From the cage he was quickly transferred to the Combined Services Detailed Interrogation Centre at Trent Park in north London, a more elaborate set-up where various rooms were bugged to record prisoners' conversations. Following interrogation, he was moved to the first (and at the time only) officers' PoW camp at Grizedale Hall in the Lake District. Here von Werra planned and carried out his first escape, absconding from a poorly guarded work party and hiding out in a shepherd's hut. After a few days on the run his hiding place was surrounded and he was finally discovered concealed in a large puddle of mud. Following his recapture, von Werra was not taken back to Grizedale Hall but instead transferred to Hayes Camp in Swanwick, Derbyshire, based around the large country house called Swanwick Hayes, now a Christian conference and education centre.

At the Hayes, von Werra became part of a group of prisoners who dubbed themselves 'Swanwick Tiefbau A.G.', or Swanwick Excavations Inc., devoted to the digging of escape tunnels. In December 1940, after a month of digging with spoons, the tunnel was complete, running 30 metres from a bedroom, under the security fence and out into the countryside. On the night of the planned escape von Werra and several companions made their way through the tunnel and out, hoping to use false documents to make good their escape. Some hoped to board a neutral ship, but von Werra's plan was more daring: posing as a downed Dutch pilot, he talked his way into an air-base, RAF Hucknall, and managed to climb inside an aircraft, hoping to fly home. While trying to learn the controls, he was arrested at gunpoint and escorted back to the Hayes.

Many of the sites like Grizedale Hall and the Hayes that served as PoW camps preserve traces of their former use: graffiti, signage and other marks reveal their wartime history. At the Hayes, however, Swanwick Excavation Inc. left a rather more substantial reminder of their presence: the 30-metre escape tunnel is still intact – an icon in the archaeology of prisoners of war.

Like many or most German PoWs in the years before D-Day, von Werra was transferred by boat to Canada, sailing in January 1941 for a camp likely to be more secure and more remote than any of his temporary homes in Britain. In a daring escape, von Werra and seven other prisoners jumped from a train outside Montreal, with the hope of making their way to the US, then still a neutral country. While the others were recaptured, von Werra was able to flee across the frozen St Lawrence River and arrived in the US to become a press and propaganda sensation. After a circuitous journey through Latin America and southern Europe, von Werra arrived back in Germany to a rapturous welcome, the only German PoW to make a home run from Allied captivity in the war. Von Werra rejoined the Luftwaffe, making several more kills on the Eastern Front. In October 1941 his aircraft disappeared over the North Sea near Holland, probably due to engine failure. No trace of von Werra was ever found.

A History of German PoWs in the Second World War

The treatment of German PoWs by Allied forces was generally but not uniformly good, but it was characterised by a strange paranoia. German prisoners were regarded somewhat like radioactive material: as a useful and valuable resource but also as a potential hazard. Thus they were kept securely stored and shipped carefully about the world. Until the invasion of Europe in June 1944 there were relatively few German PoWs in Britain. While tens of thousands were captured in North Africa during this period, the only prisoners in Britain were U-boat or merchant marine sailors captured in British waters, and Luftwaffe crew shot down over Britain. The number of prisoners was tiny: in March 1940 there were just 257, and up to June 1944 the numbers fluctuated between just 200 and, at most, 2,500, with groups of several hundred being shipped to remote Canadian PoW camps at regular intervals. Following D-Day the numbers of prisoners rose rapidly: to around 90,000 in September 1944 and a peak of 402,200 two years later.

The treatment of PoWs in the Second World War was governed by the Third Geneva Convention of 1929, to which both Britain and Germany (but not Japan or the Soviet Union) were signatories. The convention laid out a number of rules for the location, form and standard of PoW camps, as well as the types of work that prisoners could carry out, the amounts and types of food they should receive, and the circumstances (such as ill-health) under which prisoners should be repatriated. The maintenance of these standards and the administration of prisoners' post and contact between the belligerent nations was coordinated by the International Committee of the Red Cross.

Under the terms of the Geneva Convention PoWs were required to be housed at a safe distance from the front lines, and this was used as a (somewhat tenuous) rationale for the shipping of German PoWs to camps in Canada: the simultaneous importation of Italian PoWs into Britain as agricultural labourers rather undermined this argument. The Convention also required the living conditions in PoW camps to be comparable to that in the host nation's own barracks; thus in many camps the prisoners' huts are physically indistinguishable from the guards' accommodation on the other side of the wire. Prisoners were supposed to be given culturally appropriate food, although this was not always possible. German PoWs in Texas complained that they did not receive cabbages, and many in Britain found white or wholemeal bread too soft and indigestible compared to the heavy black bread they were accustomed to. While officer prisoners could not be compelled to work, other ranks could, although they were not permitted to work in war-related activities such as building airfields or manufacturing armaments. Most PoWs worked in agricultural jobs, while many others worked in manufacturing and construction, particularly in the post-war years. Prisoners were paid a pittance for their work: one recalled that his wages for a week's work on a farm could buy him just one bottle of lemonade and a small piece of cake.

The movement of PoWs between camps, transit camps and interrogation centres generally followed the pattern that Franz von Werra experienced: following capture, PoWs most often spent a night or two in a local police station or army camp while arrangements were made for their transfer to an interrogation 'cage' run by the Intelligence Corps. The interrogations varied in formality and friendliness, and were aimed at assessing the strength of a German prisoner's Nazi beliefs as well as extracting useful military intelligence. In some of these centres stool-pigeons were placed in the cells: British agents of German origin, wearing German uniforms and impersonating PoWs, whose aims were to extract more information than the prisoner had previously provided. Many prisoners were too cautious to give much away but a few found the opportunity to talk to a compatriot after days of solitary imprisonment irresistible. Following interrogation, the PoWs were transferred to one of the camps located around the country on race-tracks, country estates, old mills and so on. For most, up to 1944, their stay in Britain would be a short one.

The shipping of German PoWs to Canada, and later to Australia and the USA, requires some explanation. The numbers of prisoners were small and, in 1940, likely to remain so for some time. They represented a relatively minor logistical and administrative burden, and most seemed content to wait out what they expected to be a short war and a rapid German victory. There was even a precedent: in the First World War tens of thousands of German prisoners had been held in Britain without major incident, many of them working as agricultural labourers. Why, then, were the prisoners shipped to camps in Canada?

Throughout the early years of the war there was a widespread fear of spies and enemy aliens making up a 'fifth-column' of Nazi sympathisers in Britain. Combined with a fear of airborne troops and a near-hysterical fear-mongering campaign by the tabloid press, there was a widespread belief that German nationals and German PoWs in Britain presented a real and immediate threat. Questions were asked in Parliament about the viability of German paratroopers dropping men and weapons into PoW camps. The Geneva Convention specifically forbade the moving of PoWs outside the theatre of war in which they were captured, but the British government argued that Canada did not count as a separate country. On 21 June 1940 the SS *Duchess of York* sailed from Liverpool with 500 PoWs – the first of many such transatlantic shipments of prisoners. Within two years, while shipments of German PoWs to Canada continued, Italian PoWs captured in North Africa were being shipped into the UK in their tens of thousands to work in agriculture, utterly negating the Foreign Office's claim that PoWs were being evacuated out of Britain to protect them from air raids.

The widespread fear of German PoWs as a potential threat to national security or as an 'enemy within' appears somewhat absurd in retrospect, particularly in view of the generally placid nature of post-1944 German PoWs and the relatively light security required in PoW camps, especially when compared to German PoW camps. However, in 1940, with the fall of France and the evacuation of the BEF from Dunkirk, these threats must have seemed more realistic. In a sense the spectre of the liberated and armed PoW is just one of many perceived threats to Britain in the Second World War that never emerged, alongside in-vasion and the use of poison gas. In all of these cases preparations were made that endure into the present: thousands of anti-invasion defences survive in British coastal regions and inland, and tens of millions of gas masks were distributed to the population and returned, years later, unused. In a sense the archaeological remains of the Second World War in Britain are as much a record of imagined or perceived threats as of real ones.

In 1944, as the Allied armies advanced across western Europe, the numbers of German PoWs began to grow to tens and later hundreds of thousands. Within three months the number housed in the UK had grown from 8,000 to 90,000. By the end of the war this number had more than doubled. This sudden influx of prisoners caused a number of prac-tical problems and forced the creation of a large number of PoW camps of the type more familiar in popular culture: huts in rows, surrounded by barbed wire. Many of the camps used for German PoWs had previ-ously served as army camps in the run-up to D-Day, as temporary housing for war workers, or as camps for Italian PoWs. This last group presented something of a problem: brought to Britain from North Africa to work in agriculture, they numbered some 140,000 in late 1944. After Italy's surrender in September 1943 and its declaration of war on Germany, the status of the Italian PoWs became ambiguous, but the British government was keen to keep them as cheap and plentiful labour. A new designation of 'co-operator' was devised for Italians willing to stay in Britain in improved conditions, which included moving out of camps into billets. Many of these newly available camps were used to house German PoWs.

As the number of Italian PoWs in Britain fell and the number of Germans grew, the government grudgingly consented to allowing some German PoWs to work outside their camps: initially only a small number employed in forestry and agriculture. The success of this experiment meant that in late 1944 more than 65,000 German PoWs were at work in Britain, and the demand from employers for this cheap labour appeared insatiable. After the end of the war more and more German PoWs were brought to Britain to work on reconstruction projects as well as in agriculture, engineering and other essential areas. The repatriation of prisoners to Germany began in 1946 and ended in mid-1948. Around 25,000 German PoWs decided to remain in Britain; some had married local women, others had no homes to return to, or preferred not to return to East Germany or the regions of Germany ceded to Poland. The hundreds of camps that had held prisoners across Britain were gradually emptied and demolished, sold, re-used or forgotten. Some retained their form more or less complete; others were erased and buried under expanding towns. The PoW camps – never built with permanence in mind – have left a varied set of remains in the archaeology and heritage of Second World War Britain.

Life in a PoW Camp

Given the range of sites that were used or reused as PoW camps, it is hard to describe the appearance of a 'typical' camp. However, the sites that were constructed in the latter part of the war for the fast-growing numbers of German PoWs followed a number of set patterns and layouts, and were made up of similar types of building. What compli-cates the study of PoW camps for the archaeologist is how closely they resemble army camps, labour camps, displaced person camps, transit camps and, in other contexts, concentration camps and slave labour camps: the pattern of huts, a fence or wall, a parade area, centralised washing and eating facilities, and a central command building are common to all of these.

The PoW camp for German prisoners in Britain in the period 1944–48 typically consisted of thirty or more huts, laid out in a grid pattern with an open space around them and the whole surrounded by barbed wire fences. Outside the prisoners' area there would be a smaller enclosure for the guards' accommodation, and an administrative block for the commandant's office and other facilities. Many camps had a space set aside for sports, either within the main enclosure or appended to it, where prisoners played football and other activities (the famous Manchester City goalkeeper Bert Trautmann was held as a PoW in Lancashire, settling in the area after his release in 1948. In the 1956 FA Cup Final he played to the end despite breaking his neck in the second half.)

The layout of the camp with spaces between the huts allowed for movement and better ventilation, as well as allowing the guards to see clearly across the camp and observe the prisoners' behaviour. Few PoW camps in Britain had the guard towers familiar from films of Stalag Luft III and Colditz, and security was generally less vigilant than in German camps. As well as residential huts, holding up to fifty prisoners, there were huts for showers, washbasins and toilets, an infirmary, dining halls, kitchens, and often huts used as chapels, theatres, music rooms and lecture halls. The huts themselves varied in construction, with several common types, most of which were also used in army camps and other installations. The 4.8 metre-wide Nissen hut, formed of curved sheets of corrugated iron with brick or wooden end walls, was a common feature of PoW camps. They were built of 1.8 metre segments and could be constructed in a range of sizes. A similarly curved but slightly wider structure was commonly constructed out of corrugated asbestos, and both these and the Nissen hut (where they have survived) are still commonly used in agriculture. Another, less resilient, type of building was the Ministry of Supply Living Hut, a wood and plasterboard pre-fabricated structure that could be assembled quickly and easily, but was not designed for long-term use. Finally, many PoW camps consisted of temporary brick or breezeblock rectangular buildings with corrugated iron or asbestos roofs. The interiors of the huts were laid out in different patterns depending on their uses, with barracks typically divided into smaller rooms for eight or more prisoners, or for smaller numbers in officers' camps. In these insalubrious surroundings the prisoners passed months and years in one another's company, most leaving the camp only to work. The world within the wire was one of boredom and routine, broken up where possible by activities and entertainment, and occasional attempts to escape.

One of the biggest problems facing PoWs was depression and other forms of mental illness brought on by a sense of boredom, frustration and a desire to return to take part in the war. The sense of imprisonment without end combined with the normal friction of people living in close proximity further exacerbated these issues. For these reasons prisoners were encouraged to take part in activities and diversions of various kinds, and facilities for these were provided by the Red Cross as well as by some more enlightened camp commandants. Musical instruments were often made available, and some camps were able to put together reasonably decent ensembles. Sporting equipment such as footballs were often provided by the Red Cross, although the prisoners in one camp in the US complained that the balls kept bursting on the barbed wire. Where space was available, some prisoners cultivated gardens, either to augment their diets or to create a feeling of homeliness in the camp. Some camps possessed the facilities to create newspapers, and these were popular forums for gossip, poetry and news. The political activities and proclivities of the prisoners were of great interest to the camp authorities, as committed Nazis were considered a greater escape risk. Some camps had relatively apolitical populations content to sit out the war but in others, particularly those holding SS men captured after D-Day, some of the prisoners would enforce Nazi ideology within the PoW population. In these cases PoWs who spoke out against the Nazi leadership or suggested that Germany might lose the war were subjected to violent punishments.

Alongside sports and music, many PoWs practised or developed artistic talents in captivity, painting pictures on the walls of their huts and transforming everyday objects such as mess tins and mugs into intricate works of art. Craft products such as toys and wood carvings were often gifted or sold to people living near the camps, or to the people who employed PoWs. Many of these objects are still held in museums and private collections – another part of the enduring heritage of the half-million or more prisoners of war who made up part of Britain's wartime population.

Some prisoners who found their confinement unbearable turned their attention to the activity most commonly associated with PoWs: escaping. While Franz von Werra was the only German PoW to make a successful home run, many others attempted to escape by tunnelling or tricking their way out of their camps. Like von Werra's tunnel at Swanwick, some of these escape attempts have left traces in the archaeology and built heritage of the camp sites.

Island Farm and the Welsh Great Escape

In the early 1980s in Bridgend, Wales, Reg Dodson made a surprising discovery. A police officer and history buff, Dodson had long been fascinated by the Island Farm PoW camp in Bridgend and the lives of the prisoners there. While exploring one of the concrete buildings on the site, he found that the end of one room had been cunningly sealed off by an improvised false wall. Behind the wall Dodson found a 2 metre-high heap of old, dried balls of clay – and the answer to the riddle that had puzzled the guards at Island Farm in 1945: where had the prisoners hidden the soil from their escape tunnel?

Prisoner of War Camp 198 at Island Farm, Bridgend, was the site of the most daring PoW escape in Second World War Britain – the so-called 'Welsh Great Escape', which saw seventy German PoWs tunnel out of the camp and disperse across the countryside, although all were eventually recaptured. Island Farm camp was not built as a PoW camp: in 1938 a branch of the Royal Ordnance Factory was established at Bridgend, forming part of a vast network of armaments manufacturing that, at its peak, employed more than 40,000 people, mostly in shell manufacture. This enormous enterprise drew its workforce from the surrounding area, and so, to ease the long commute that some workers had to make, the Royal Ordnance Factory built a camp of wooden huts on land belonging to Island Farm close to the factory. The camp proved unpopular with the largely female workforce, who preferred a long commute to and from their homes rather than accommodation in draughty wooden huts, and so the camp lay empty for several years until late 1943, when it was used to house troops of the US Army's 28th Infantry Division in preparation for D-Day.

Soon after D-Day, as the number of German PoWs captured in Europe grew, the Island Farm camp was converted into a PoW camp and given the number 198. Early prisoners were put to work improving and securing the camp, and by late 1944 the camp held several hundred prisoners, most of them officers and many of them members of the Waffen SS. In January 1945 the camp guards discovered a tunnel being excavated from one of the huts, where prisoners had removed part of a hearth to access the earth and construct a tunnel. The tunnel that was eventually used in the Welsh Great Escape began from Hut 9, one of the buildings closest to the wire. Such was the secrecy surrounding the escape that it is still unclear who the ringleaders and planners were.

The tunnel from Hut 9 descended vertically for almost 3 metres, then turned towards the wire. The tunnel itself was around a metre square, shored up with stolen pieces of wood, and reaching a length of 18 metres in total. Ventilation was a common problem in tunnelling (as Franz von Werra discovered) and, as in the original Great Escape, the prisoners found that dried milk tins from their Red Cross parcels could be joined together to form air pipes for a makeshift pump to keep the excavators alive. Soil and clay from the tunnel was disposed of in a cunning manner, not discovered until the 1980s: a false wall was constructed at the end of a large L-shaped room, and the cavity was gradually filled with the clay and earth, formed into small balls for ease of disguise and disposal. The tunnel was lit with electric light drawn from the hut's wiring, and lights were used as signals to warn of the approach of guards.

On the night of 10 March 1945 the tunnel was complete and the escapers had prepared forged documents and civilian clothing, and had organised distractions within the camp to cover their escape. Some prisoners on work parties in the surrounding area had scouted out hiding places and resources such as a car parked near the camp which could be (and was) stolen. After the evening roll-call had been completed, the prisoners taking part in the escape arrived at Hut 9 in dribs and drabs to avoid attracting attention, and began to make their way through the tunnel and out of the camp. Seventy prisoners made their escape through the tunnel, and fanned out across the country-side. Four prisoners stole the small Austin car belonging to a local doctor, and with the unwitting help of some passing PoW camp guards they managed to push-start the vehicle. They drove east with the aim of reaching Croydon airfield and stealing an aircraft, but ran out of fuel before reaching Gloucester and abandoned the vehicle. After sneaking on to a goods train and taking shelter in a field, they were discovered and captured in Castle Bromwich near Birmingham.

By this time most of the prisoners had been apprehended: many of them around the tunnel exit after the alarm was raised, and others in the local area. Two prisoners hid on a goods train, but it was travelling slowly and in the wrong direction for the escapees, who had hoped to reach a port. They were captured just a few miles from the camp. Two other prisoners managed to climb aboard a goods train to Southampton but were apprehended some 120 miles from the camp, the furthest that any of the escapers reached. The hue and cry had gone out, and police and local military units had carried out pre-arranged processes for an escape including road-blocks, searches of abandoned buildings, and – in one place – the ringing of church-bells, which Churchill had decreed should be reserved as a signal of German invasion. The escapees were eventually all recaptured.

Following the end of the war, Camp 198 was used as a special camp to house high-profile PoWs such as Field Marshals von Rundstedt and von Manstein. In April 1948 the last prisoners were repatriated to Germany, apart from a few who had married local women, and the camp was abandoned. Over the following decades a number of local historians took an interest in the camp and a great deal of information has been gathered relating to the various stages of its use. In the 1980s it was interest in the history of the camp that led to the discovery of the hidden compartment where earth from the tunnel was concealed. In the early 1990s the concrete buildings on the site were demolished, and most traces of the camp were lost. However, the paintings on the walls of the huts were noted and preserved as a record of the prisoners' creativity.

Most importantly, Hut 9, where the escape originated, was preserved as a listed building, its historical significance being recognised. In 2003 the tunnel that ran from Hut 9 and under the wire at Island Farm was located using ground penetrating radar and a mechanical digger was used to excavate it. The roof was breached with the digger and a survey showed that the tunnel remained largely intact beneath the soil, with the wooden support structure still in place almost sixty years after its installation. The entrance shaft had collapsed slightly, but the overall condition of the tunnel was a testament to the skill of its construction. The archaeology of the Welsh Great Escape offers us a glimpse of just how much we can still learn about the lives of Axis PoWs from the traces that they left behind.

Wynches Camp

Digging in his flower bed in Much Hadham, Hertfordshire, in 2009, plumber David Murray unearthed a fragment of metal. Upon inspection, this small shiny rectangle turned out to be a German prisoner of war's dog-tag – the first clue that the garden lay on the site of a former PoW camp. His curiosity sparked by this find, Murray began to explore the garden and surrounding land with a metal-detector, eventually uncovering several pits containing a mixture of refuse and military materials. Together with a local historian, he began to record the finds and investigate the history of the site. The artefact count stands at more than 5,000 and ranges from buttons and bottles to paperwork, biscuits and a live hand-grenade.

Wynches Camp, as it was originally known, began life in 1939 as an army camp, spread over 40 acres of ground. Work on the camp proceeded slowly, and by mid-1940 the lack of Nissen huts meant that troops supposedly stationed at the camp were housed in tents. While historical sources are sparse, it seems that during the war the camp served a number of purposes, including housing Gurkha troops during their training, and later being used as a transit camp for American troops in the run-up to D-Day. The Suffolk Regiment and the Seaforth Highlanders are known to have stayed at Wynches Camp. Following D-Day, the camp was used for some time as low-security accommodation for Italian PoWs working in agriculture in the surrounding area. While there is some evidence that it was then used as a reception centre for Allied PoWs returning from captivity in Germany, the next known use was as a camp for German PoWs deemed low-risk, who were held there from 1946 to 1948, many of them employed by the Hertfordshire War Agricultural Executive Committee. During this time Wynches Camp was given the PoW camp number 411. Following its abandonment, the camp was pulled down by the army in 1950 and the land was used for a housing development.

The finds from the site indicate that pits were dug during the demolition of the camp to dispose of rubbish left behind in the huts and elsewhere. Some of the pits may have been dug for waste disposal during the life of the camp. The enormous variety of finds tells us something about life in the camps and the different groups who lived there from 1940 to 1948. Many of the finds relate to food and drink, a common source of rubbish throughout history. Much of the diet of the camp residents – whether army or PoWs – was made up of canned food, and the remains of these tins abound in the archaeology. Other food-related finds include a Sainsbury's fish-paste jar, a frying pan, cutlery, soft drinks bottles and bottle stoppers, and a biscuit tin with some of the biscuits remaining. Other artefacts attest to the residents' concerns for their grooming and health, such as combs, toothbrushes, razor blades and an assortment of medicine bottles, some of them military issue.

It is the distinctively military artefacts that can tell the most about the different uses of Wynches Camp in the Second World War. Some are standard British military issue items such as canteens, mess tins, anti-gas ointment and boots, while others are more distinctive: Murray has unearthed a number of regimental pins and badges as well as uniform buttons which can reveal which forces were stationed or held at the camp. These include a Gurkha shoulder bar, a Luftwaffe cap badge, a Suffolk Regiment cap badge, and American and British buttons. Other stray finds included American boot polish and German military issue water bottles. There were also traces of the weapons used by the soldiers stationed at the camp. A considerable number of bullets were discovered, including some that had not been fired. These were of .303 calibre, used by the British military Lee Enfield rifle and some machine guns, and .45 calibre ammunition as used in handguns and the Thompson sub-machine gun. In addition, Murray unearthed a live hand-grenade, which was reported to the police and subsequently inspected by an RAF bomb disposal team, who deemed it unstable and blew it up. Alongside these rather lethal finds were pieces of mortar shells and part of another hand-grenade. Finds such as these are a reminder of the dangers facing archaeologists examining sites of these periods, and the need to know and recognise the health and safety issues and the legal dimensions to such finds – in general, extreme caution and expert intervention are the best policies!

The numerous dog-tags discovered on the site are of particular interest, as they offer the most direct connection between artefacts and the people who used them. Many of the tags are legible, and record names such as that of US serviceman Edwin D. Haskins, as does the ID card of PoW Erhard Wolfsdorf. Several of the dog-tags are from German PoW camps and record numbers rather than names; in some cases it may be possible to connect these to individual names through historical research. The team working on the site of Wynches Camp are trying to contact people who may have been stationed or held as prisoners at the camp between 1940 and 1948 and who might be able to shed more light on the history of the site.

At Wynches Camp there is little to see above the ground – the demolition of the site was near-total, and only the remains of one Nissen hut survive. The researchers are using aerial photographs to trace the original locations of the huts on the site, and to find the likely locations of more rubbish pits with their rich harvest of artefacts that reveal the minute details of the camp's inhabitants: their names, what they ate and drank, and the everyday things they used to eat, wash and work. In one sense the rubbish pits are archaeological treasure troves, but in another sense they are a bit of a mess: by jumbling all the artefacts into pits the demolition teams of 1950 have made it much harder for twenty-first-century archaeologists to learn about the site. On most archaeological sites the sequence of events is revealed in the layers of material deposited in the ground, the lower layers being the oldest, and the uppermost being the more recent. Where objects have been mixed up before burial, it is hard for the archaeologist to know which objects represent the earliest phases of the site and which are the latest. Fortunately at Wynches Camp there is sufficient historical data to reconstruct many of the episodes in the life of the site that for a few years served as Prisoner of War Camp 411.

Harperley Camp

Harperley Camp in County Durham, formerly PoW Camp 93, is one of the best preserved surviving prisoner of war camps in Britain. It was recently declared a scheduled monument in recognition of its historical significance and its value as a heritage site. The camp was constructed in 1943 as Prisoner of War Camp 93, and held several hundred Italian PoWs in low-security conditions. The camp consisted of around seventy buildings on a 12 acre site on the side of a hill; most of the buildings were Ministry of War Supply Standard Huts. These used prefabricated concrete frames and walls of brick or breezeblock, with roofs made of asbestos sheeting. From 1944 to 1948 the camp housed up to 900 German PoWs at any one time, all of them deemed low-risk and many of them employed in agricultural work in the area. Following the closure of the PoW camp the land reverted to the ownership of the farm that it had been requisitioned from, and for a short time some of the buildings were used for agricultural storage and as chicken sheds, before again falling out of use. This abandonment means that Harperley Camp is one of the best preserved PoW camps in the world.

Life in the camp was largely focused on work, but time was set aside for educational activities, including 'De-Nazification' classes which aimed to teach the merits of democracy to the prisoners (many of whom had grown up in the Third Reich). The PoWs produced a camp newspaper entitled *Der Quell*, and other cultural activities were encouraged. A small orchestra was formed, as well as a dramatic society, and both put on regular productions. One of the most remarkable survivals in the camp today is the theatre: within the confines of a normal camp hut, the prisoners created a miniature theatre complete with banked seating, a prompt box, orchestra pit, wall decoration and a proscenium arch. Here the prisoners staged concerts and other events, including a series of comedies. The other remarkable survival is the dining hall, where a series of elaborate wall paintings survive in situ: these were painted by one of the prisoners, and show a variety of classic German landscape views. This building was used by the prisoners as a relaxation area outside their residential huts. Alongside these cultural activities, the prisoners also had a football pitch, and a team of prisoners occasionally played competitive matches against local teams. Another activity that prisoners used to pass the time was craft production, including carving wooden toys and other products, many of which were sold to local people. There was light security at the site and escaping did not feature among the prisoners' activities – in the life of the camp only one PoW attempted to abscond.

In 1999 the site was purchased by a local couple, the McLeods, who hoped to restore the camp and turn it into a heritage attraction. Together with English Heritage, they put together a management plan that included the scheduling of the site as a historic monument, and in 2003 Harperley Camp featured on a BBC restoration programme, reaching the semi-final but failing to win the cash prize to help preserve the buildings. By 2009 the McLeods had run out of money and put the entire site up for sale on eBay, where it failed to sell. In 2011, with prospects for the site's survival looking poor, English Heritage awarded it half a million pounds. This money is intended to restore the theatre and canteen buildings only, which will be enclosed in temporary structures while repairs and conservation work take place. It is hoped that with the unique theatre and the remarkable wall paintings preserved, Harperley Camp will continue to serve as a reminder of the prisoner of war experience in Second World War Britain: a uniquely well preserved trace of the network of hundreds of PoW camps in wartime and post-war Britain.

The Future of PoW Archaeology and Heritage

The surviving traces of the escape tunnels at Swanwick and at Island Farm, the tumbled pits of artefacts at Wynches Camp and the wall paintings at Harperley Camp are all part of the archaeology and the heritage of prisoners of war in Second World War Britain. This population of more than half a million made a significant contribution to British industry and agriculture during the war and into the post-war era, and tens of thousands of them stayed to become naturalised British citizens. Today their history is largely forgotten, and the number of surviving former PoWs with memories of the camps grows smaller every year. The burden of memory falls ever more strongly on the artefacts and sites that remain, but these too are under threat. Most of the Island Farm site was needlessly bulldozed, and barely any trace remains above ground at Wynches Camp. Even Harperley Camp with its astonishing levels of survival – particularly for buildings meant to be temporary structures with a very short lifespan – is now threatened by decay and lack of funds to preserve anything other than the most significant structures on the site.

This theme of rapid creation and destruction, of temporary buildings and ephemeral sites not meant to last, is one that permeates the PoW story in the Second World War. As witnessed by the secret tunnels and false wall uncovered by more recent studies of these camps, the PoW experience was one of hidden experiences and subtle acts of resistance. The archaeologists of the future will no doubt uncover a great deal more about the hidden and forgotten lives of the prisoners of war, throwing light on their stories of endurance, hope and survival. As David Murray, the excavator of the Wynches Camp site remarked, 'The Second World War might be recent history – but how often in life do you get the chance to find all this before it's gone and to do the research and get people's stories before they're gone as well?'

Further Reading

Burt, Kendal and James Leasor, *The One That Got Away* (Pen & Sword, 2006)

Clay, Catrine, *Trautmann's Journey: From Hitler Youth to FA Cup Legend* (Yellow Jersey Press, 2011)

Cocroft, Wayne, Danielle Devlin, John Schofield and Roger J.C. Thomas, *War Art* (Council for British Archaeology, 2006)

Edwards, Gloria, *Moota – Camp 103: The Story of a Cumbrian Prisoner of War Camp* (Little Bird Publications, 2003)

Howe Taylor, Pamela, *The Germans We Trusted* (Lutterworth Press, 2003)

Jackson, Sophie, *Churchill's Unexpected Guests: Prisoners of War in Britain in World War II* (History Press, 2010)

Risby, Stephen, *Prisoners of War in Bedfordshire* (Amberley, 2011)

Waters, Michael, *Lone Star Stalag: German Prisoners of War at Camp Hearne* (Texas A&M University Press, 2004)

Useful Websites

www.islandfarm.fsnet.co.uk

A detailed history of Island Farm Prisoner of War camp in Bridgend, Wales, including a great deal of historical material and copies of old photographs.

wynchescamp411.co.uk

Updates on the excavations and research into Wynches Camp in Much Hadham, Hertfordshire, including images of the artefacts and the site.

Places to Visit

Eden Camp Modern History Theme Museum

Eden Camp is a Second World War theme museum housed in a former prisoner of war camp near Malton, North Yorkshire. The museum covers various aspects of the history of the war, including the Blitz and Bomber Command, and the site itself is one of the best preserved PoW camps in the country.

Eden Camp Modern History Theme Museum
Malton
North Yorkshire
YO17 6RT
www.edencamp.co.uk

Chapter 5

The RAF Crewman

In 2004 Channel Five screened live the excavation of a Hawker Hurricane fighter aircraft from beneath a street in central London. Years of planning and research by aviation archaeologist Christopher Bennett had led to this remarkable moment: the raising of the Rolls-Royce Merlin engine from the London clay, broadcast live, as a large crowd gathered around the site. And there to see it emerge was Ray Holmes, getting his first glimpse of the aircraft he had last seen more than sixty years earlier as he drifted to earth in his parachute.

In 1940, at the height of the Battle of Britain, Sergeant Holmes of 504 Squadron had spotted a Dornier Do17 while on patrol over London. He gave chase to the bomber, which appeared to be heading for Buckingham Palace. Having fired away all of his ammunition to little effect, Sergeant Holmes was left with no option but to ram his single-engined Hurricane into the much larger bomber, sending it spinning to earth at the front of Victoria station, where it exploded. The Hurricane was badly damaged in the collision but Holmes had baled out moments before the impact, allowing the aircraft to fall to earth on the corner of Buckingham Palace Road, where the half-ton weight of the Merlin engine drove the wreckage deep into the ground.

More than sixty years later the 89-year-old watched from his wheelchair as pieces of the aircraft were brought to light: small fragments of the airframe of aluminium, steel, wood and doped fabric; pieces of the radio and cockpit fittings, and, most movingly of all, the control column of the Hurricane. The circular spade-grip of this was found with the brass gun button still set to the 'fire' position. In front of the television cameras, Ray Holmes, frail and quiet, refused to be treated as a hero, insisting that he had just done his duty.

The stories of the Battle of Britain, the Blitz, the bombing of Germany and the achievements and sacrifices of the Royal Air Force in general are well known, but there are still new stories to bring to light that illuminate the human dimensions of this conflict and to teach the familiar stories to new generations. The archaeology of the Royal Air Force and the people who served in it is a vital part of the story of the Second World War: the remains of the aircraft, the airfields that they flew from and the men who flew in them are among the most important parts of Britain's wartime heritage, worthy of study and protection.

Background

In the aftermath of the First World War the young Royal Air Force had found its greatest role in policing the empire, bombing villages in, among other places, Iraq and Afghanistan. From the early 1920s the strength of the RAF at home began to grow as well, in response to government committee recommendations about the defence of the nation against bombing – as well as the ability to project bomber forces into Europe. Under these plans a network of fighter bases and other defences would protect the capital, and some First World War airfields were brought back into service. In the 1930s the most obvious future threat was German rearmament, and a series of RAF Expansion Schemes sought to match this. This led to a rapid expansion in airfield construction, aircraft manufacture, and ground and air training. From 1934 the scheme was expanded with the aim by 1939 of raising the strength of the RAF to 111 front-line squadrons and another sixteen of the Fleet Air Arm (then under RAF control): a total of around 1,500 aircraft. Alongside this growth in brute strength, there were technological advances taking place: experiments aimed at creating an anti-aircraft death-ray failed, but they led to a more useful defensive weapon – radar. The first experiments took place in 1935, and by 1940 the network of radar stations along the coasts were a vital component in Britain's air defence, playing a significant part in winning the Battle of Britain. The few surviving radar sites from this early period are justly considered among the most valuable elements of wartime heritage.

In 1936 the RAF Air Defence of Great Britain was divided into separate commands, reflecting the different roles that it was expected to play. The new groupings were Fighter Command, Bomber Command, Coastal Command and Training Command. At the same time the RAF Volunteer Reserve was formed, making training available to all regardless of social class: many future RAF aircrew of the Second World War were trained under this scheme and helped to build up the depth of experienced crew that would remain one of the most valuable and often scarce resources throughout the war.

Throughout the Second World War the RAF took part in campaigns around the world, from the defence of Malta and the struggle for North Africa to Ceylon, Norway and Russia. Aircraft of the RAF took part in the sinkings of *Bismarck* and *Tirpitz,* and supported ground and sea actions including the evacuation of Dunkirk, the Normandy landings and the invasion of Italy. In this chapter, however, I am concentrating on RAF aircraft operating out of airfields in Britain, and focusing in particular on two of the most notable episodes in the history of air warfare: the Battle of Britain, where RAF fighters defended cities and their own bases from German bombers; and the large-scale strategic bombing campaign against Germany by RAF and USAAF aircraft from 1942.

Fighter Command and the Battle of Britain

In the late 1930s RAF Fighter Command replaced most of its relatively lightly armed biplanes with more modern aircraft, most notably two eight-gun monoplane fighters: the Hawker Hurricane and the Supermarine Spitfire. By the outbreak of war the Hurricane was the most numerous, with numbers of Spitfires rising rapidly, alongside smaller numbers of other types such as the Boulton-Paul Defiant, with its rear-facing gun turret armament, and the fighter version of the Bristol Blenheim light bomber. Both of these types suffered heavy losses throughout 1940 and were switched to mainly night-fighting duties.

RAF Fighter Command operated an elaborate system of command and control, based on a network of observation and detection systems and a well coordinated communication network. Information on incoming German air raids was gathered from radar readings and Observer Corps reports and relayed to a central operations centre, from which the relevant information was dispatched to the four Fighter Groups with responsibility for different sectors of British airspace. The ability to gather, filter and transmit intelligence on German movements was crucial to the RAF's success in combating the German bombers, as it allowed Fighter Command to respond to specific threats with optimal force rather than mounting wasteful and inefficient standing air patrols.

The lead-up to the Battle of Britain saw the Luftwaffe attack British shipping in the Channel, as well as the Channel ports, including Portsmouth. From the summer of 1940 the Germans recognised the need to establish air superiority over southern Britain and the Channel if the planned invasion of Britain, codenamed Operation Sea Lion, were to succeed. From August 1940 they began to focus their attacks on Fighter Command airfields in southern England, as well as radar stations and aircraft manufacturing centres such as the Supermarine factory in Southampton. This period saw many RAF airfields such as Hawkinge in Kent and Tangmere in Sussex nearly reduced to ruins, and both the RAF and the Luftwaffe suffered heavy losses. While both sides sped up aircraft production to make up for combat losses, the most valuable resource was trained pilots: training a pilot to replace those killed, injured or taken prisoner took considerably longer than replacing aircraft, but here the RAF had the advantage of fighting over their own territory, so that pilots who survived a crash-landing or parachute descent could usually be returned to operational flying quickly.

In late August 1940 there were raids by the Luftwaffe on London, and by the RAF on Berlin. Enraged by the latter, Hitler ordered the Luftwaffe to switch their attacks to British cities, bringing the horrors of the Blitz to London, Coventry and other cities, but giving Fighter Command the respite it needed to restore its strength and rally against the German raiders. From September 1940 the Luftwaffe pounded London relentlessly for months of day and night raids, but the enduring strength of the RAF and its ability to conduct efficient defences against a weakening Luftwaffe gradually convinced Hitler not to invade Britain, with Operation Sea Lion first postponed and then shelved indefinitely.

By the end of October 1940 the Battle of Britain had been won by RAF Fighter Command. Although bombing raids on British cities continued to intensify through the winter of 1940/41, the Germans had decisively failed to establish air superiority over Britain and invasion had been averted. The exact casualty figures for the battle are disputed, with inaccurate reporting on both sides, but conservative estimates place RAF losses at around 1,000 aircraft and some 540 crew, and Luftwaffe losses at around 1,900 aircraft and some 2,700 crew. It is worth noting that the majority of RAF losses were single-engined fighter aircraft, while many of the German casualties were twin-engined bombers with crews of up to five. Across southern and eastern Britain the remains of these aircraft and men were scattered in ruins: some, like Ray Holmes' Hurricane, were buried deep in the ground. Others came to rest on the surface in relatively intact condition; many (particularly German aircraft) came down in the Channel. The wrecks of aircraft littered the beaches, fields, hills and streets of Britain that Churchill had pledged to defend. Among the wreckage lay the remains of hundreds of men: some recovered at the time and buried with military honours, others lost or forgotten.

Bomber Command and the Strategic Bombing of Germany

At the outbreak of the Second World War RAF Bomber Command was in no shape to take the war to the enemy, but neither was it expected to. Informal agreements between the combatant nations restricted bombing to military targets and key infrastructure but forbade the bombing of urban areas. Bomber Command's fleet largely consisted of slow and vulnerable light and medium bombers such as the Fairey Battle, Armstrong-Whitworth Whitley and Handley-Page Hampden. Even the more advanced types, such as the Vickers Wellington and Bristol Blenheim, were outdated by the outbreak of war. At this point the more advanced heavy bombers, such as the Handley-Page Halifax and Avro Lancaster, were still on the drawing-boards.

In the early months of the war Bomber Command dropped millions of propaganda leaflets over German cities, bombed coastal installations, including invasion barges, and dropped mines around German ports and naval sites. In France the RAF flew bombing missions in support of the British Expeditionary Forces. On these missions, and on the few bombing missions carried out against German cities in 1940, the RAF suffered extremely heavy losses to German fighter aircraft and to powerful and accurate anti-aircraft artillery. Following these losses on daylight raids, Bomber Command switched to overwhelmingly night-time operations, a policy that endured throughout the war, with the US Army Air Force flying day-time operations over occupied Europe from 1942.

In 1942 Bomber Command began to build up its strength and numbers of heavy bombers, following serious losses in 1941. In February 1942 the Air Ministry issued the Area Bombing Directive, ordering the RAF to attack Germany's industrial cities, including their civilian populations, with the aim of destroying Germany's means and morale to continue the war. This directive led to attacks on numerous cities, including Cologne and Essen. The attacks continued to grow in size and number, and in May 1942 the first thousand-bomber raid was carried out by the RAF against Cologne; it was a considerable propaganda coup for Bomber Command, although several obsolete types had to be drafted in to make up the numbers. In developing its policy of strategic bombing and lobbying for government support, Bomber Command employed teams of scientists to research the efficacy of different approaches. It was on the basis of these reports that Bomber Command pursued a policy of 'dehousing' the German population by destroying housing in cities. The RAF employed a range of advanced technologies such as airborne radar, radio-based navigational aids and the use of 'pathfinder' target markers to improve its bombing accuracy (which had been abysmal in the early period of night-raids, with only a tiny percentage of bombs landing within miles of the targets). From 1943 the RAF's night-bombing campaign was coordinated with the USAAF's daylight raids using the highly accurate Norden bombsight. This combination of forces had a devastating effect on German cities, although the policy of area bombing has been criticised on strategic and moral grounds.

In Britain the bombing offensive produced significant changes in the landscape and in industry. Factories and workshops across the country turned to aircraft manufacture in greater and greater numbers, with components and other resources shipped to giant assembly plants. Under the control of the Ministry of Aircraft Production, run for the last part of the war by the left-wing politician Stafford Cripps, aircraft manufacturing soared to the point that the continued bombing of Germany consumed more than a third of Britain's economic output.

Scores of new airfields were built across the eastern side of the country, with many older airfields being expanded or their runways extended to allow the new heavy bombers to operate from them. The flatter landscapes of Cambridgeshire and Lincolnshire lent themselves to airfield construction, as well as offering the shortest flying times across the North Sea to Germany. Airfields were also needed for the growing number of USAAF bomber and fighter groups operating out of Britain: in many cases existing RAF bases were used or expanded, while in other cases new bases were built in record time, with concrete runways laid alongside quickly erected Nissen huts and prefabricated hangars. The flimsiness of many of these buildings has not helped their long-term survival.

At the end of the war, as the RAF and USAAF abandoned or moth-balled most of their bases, rumours began to spread that the USAAF had left behind vast amounts of aircraft, trucks, armaments and other materials. These stories have now entered into folklore around many former airfields: USAAF men are supposed to have dug vast pits in the ground, the size of football fields and many metres deep, in which entire bomber aircraft were interred alongside brand-new motorbikes, jeeps and other tempting treasures. In the stories many of these objects are still in their delivery crates and could almost be driven out their earthy graves if excavated. Various surveys of these sites have suggested that such stories are nothing more than myths, like the Pacific islanders whose 'cargo cult' religions rest on the memory of American military munificence in the Second World War. No doubt these stories will continue to enchant treasure-seekers and archaeologists in the future, and it is possible that one day a treasure-trove of American military hardware will be uncovered – but I won't hold my breath.

RAF Airfields

The rapid expansion of the RAF home forces from the 1920s through to the outbreak of the Second World War was one of the greatest invest-ments in military infrastructure in British history. By 1939 more than fifty new permanent air-bases had been built, and a considerable number of First World War airfields had been brought up to date. Each of these airfields represented an immense amount of infrastructure and expense, from purchasing the land and laying the vast runways to the planting of flowerbeds in the residential quarters. Due to the scale of construction, a degree of standardisation was introduced, and, unlike in wartime, most buildings were constructed of permanent materials such as brick and concrete. RAF airfields were designed around the principle of dispersal, with aircraft parked around the perimeter of the airfield or in individual pens with blast walls, to prevent a surprise air attack disabling or destroying an entire base. Buildings were similarly dispersed, with tech-nical buildings, workshops and hangars arranged in a curve to prevent their destruction by a single row of bombs. Air-bases were divided into distinct sections: the flying field, the technical areas and the domestic areas. Many airstrips were grass, but in areas where the natural geology tended towards waterlogging, metalled surfaces were laid to reduce the likelihood of landing accidents. Technical areas of the air-base included control towers, hangars, training facilities, bomb and fuel storage areas, garages and workshops. Domestic structures included barracks, barbers, messes, cinemas, kitchens, laundries and married quarters. Later additions to many air-bases included extensive construction of air raid shelters, and airfield defences such as pillboxes, artillery and anti-aircraft guns.

Such a large-scale construction programme inevitably produced environmental concerns, not least among those living in close proximity to the new sites. To alleviate these concerns, the RAF worked with the Royal Fine Arts Commission to create a set of distinctive styles for airfield architecture, as well as a variety of unique and interesting structures. Domestic buildings were generally built in a neo-Georgian style with garden-city influences in the layouts, while technical buildings were overwhelmingly modernist, and control towers evolved a range of art-deco styles. Despite the widespread destruction at many sites during the Battle of Britain, as well as by more recent development and demolition, a considerable number of these 1920s and 1930s buildings have survived on former airfield sites. However, the bombing of airfields, together with the need for rapid expansion during wartime, means that many surviving airfields display a hodgepodge of buildings from different periods, many of them adapted, repaired or updated, and a mixture of temporary and permanent buildings. For example, varying numbers of pre-war and wartime hangars, such as the B1, T2 and Bellman types, survive in different places to varying degrees, some of them recognised as historically important or moved to museums and heritage sites.

Given their large number and the value of the land that they occupied, it was inevitable that many RAF and USAAF airfields would be decommissioned in the aftermath of the Second World War. For the wartime airfields carved rapidly from agricultural land, this was often a relatively rapid process. Temporary buildings such as Nissen huts and hangars were relatively easy to remove or destroy, although some were kept as storage for machinery and agricultural produce and materials.

Concrete airstrips formed useful hardstandings for the storage of certain crops and machinery, while the majority of the airfield could be fairly rapidly converted back into farmland, often leaving relatively few traces of its wartime use, at least to the untrained eye. The earlier, more permanent bases were more likely to be retained as RAF or USAF bases for the beginnings of the Cold War, while those that were decommissioned often became civilian aerodromes or were developed as industrial estates.

The historical value and interest of these wartime sites has long been recognised by the Airfield Research Group and other local and national history organisations. The Airfield Research Group brings together experts and enthusiasts with a considerable range and depth of knowledge concerning the history, architecture and archaeology of airfields, helps maintain archival sources relating to airfield history, and publishes the journal *Airfield Review* which provides updates and reports on sites around the country. Members of the Airfield Research Group were among the hundreds of volunteers who took part in the Defence of Britain Project, which recorded numerous sites and structures relating to airfields and airfield defences.

A considerable number of airfield sites that have been returned to agricultural use retain a number of original buildings; in many cases these are in poor condition, at risk of collapse and a potential hazard to those exploring them. Nevertheless they are of historical and archaeological interest, and should at least be recorded before they rot away altogether. The most common surviving buildings on these sites are those built of lasting materials such as air raid shelters and bomb storage bunkers. These are often buried, and it is the control towers that often survive most visibly, often looking rather forlorn in an empty landscape, although many have been converted into private homes.

A few airfields have been preserved, in whole or in part, as museums dedicated to the men who served there, or to the history of aviation more generally. Of these, the best known is the Imperial War Museum at Duxford: built in 1917, this airfield served with distinction in the Second World War, where Douglas Bader famously used it as a base for his 'big wing' approach to combating enemy bombers by meeting them in strength. Alongside the extraordinary collection of aircraft and associated materials, Duxford is most notable for the surviving buildings on the site, including several hangars dating back to the First World War, and the operations room where combat was plotted and controlled, reconstructed in its original wartime condition. For anyone with an interest in the archaeology of the air war, or aviation in general, Duxford is a Mecca of rare and famous aircraft types, many of them in flying condition.

Another renowned wartime airfield museum is Tangmere, also famous for its connection with Douglas Bader, as well as for its role in the Battle of Britain, when it was heavily bombed, destroying or damaging almost all of the buildings on site, including the aircraft hangars and the officers' mess. Tangmere was used extensively by SOE for transporting secret agents into occupied Europe by parachute or light aircraft. Most of the original buildings not bombed by the Luftwaffe were demolished from the 1980s onwards, but some remain, including the control tower and several hangars. Tangmere Military Aviation Museum on the site holds a small but select collection of historic aircraft, and the museum displays a considerable amount of material excavated from aircraft crash sites.

Air Crash Sites

Many years ago I was beach-combing near Brighton and came across a number of fragments of very light aluminium alloy on the high-tide mark. Most were broken rods, tubes and fragments of sheet metal but one piece, about 8cm by 5cm, had a raised edge and some numbers and letters stamped into it, reading 'Klatte Huchting'. Some research on the topic has revealed that Theodor Klatte was a manufacturer of aircraft components in Huchting, Bremen, in the Second World War. There was no doubt that the fragments of metal I had collected were part of a German aircraft, possibly a Focke-Wulf 190, that had crashed into the sea off Brighton. Either the aircraft had disintegrated on impact and fragments had been scattered about or, more likely, the relatively complete airframe was resting on the seabed some distance off the beach being slowly broken apart by waves and tides. The fragment of aluminium in my collection is an archaeological artefact, a tiny piece of history: a relic of one of the thousands of aircraft that fell from the sky around Britain during the Second World War. The excavation of these remains is aviation archaeology: one of the oldest and best established aspects of the archaeology of the Second World War in Britain, recovering and recording the remains of crashed aircraft since the 1960s.

It is hard to calculate the precise number of aircraft that crashed in wartime Britain and in the seas around it – British, German, American and also Italian aircraft, brought down by gunfire, other weapons, mechanical failure or pilot error. A conservative estimate places the number at well over 10,000 during the course of the war. Many thousands of these have left traces that archaeologists have been able to find on the crash sites years later, some clearly visible and others requiring advanced detection equipment.

In each case the precise nature of the crash has affected what was left behind for archaeologists to uncover. Aircraft that made hard, wheels-up landings on ploughed fields might have been recovered relatively undamaged, leaving behind only a few fragments of broken propeller and paint. A single-engined aircraft that fell out of control from a great height might have hit the ground nearly vertically, leaving the wings in fragments on the surface and the fuselage compacted into a lump deep beneath the ground. A larger, multi-engined aircraft might break up on impact, scattering engines, wing fragments and other major components over a wide area. Similarly the location and geology of the crash site makes a difference to what can be recovered and its likely condition. Aircraft embedded in a sandy beach or soft, marshy ground are likely to be relatively well preserved, while those that crashed into a mountain-side are likely to be found in rough fragments. Landings on water, in lakes or in the sea, were often relatively gentle and cold water can preserve metal airframes relatively well.

What is found depends also upon what recovery efforts were made at the time. The wrecks of relatively complete aircraft that landed in acces-sible areas were often collected by RAF Maintenance Units to see if they could be repaired or, at least, stripped for reusable parts and the remainder scrapped. The ruins of German aircraft were generally scrapped unless they were interesting, rare or new types, in which case they might be preserved for some time for testing. During the Battle of Britain and the Blitz aircraft fell over southern England with such regu-larity that the RAF Maintenance Units were forced to sub-contract the recovery of non-repairable aircraft wrecks to local haulage firms and garages. Inevitably, recovering broken or badly wrecked aircraft remains or fragments was not a priority for the RAF, and in many cases where wrecks were inaccessible to recovery units they were left where they fell:

this was the case for aircraft on high ground or soft ground where vehicles could not reach them, or for wreckage buried deep underground, as most recovery units had only spades to dig with.

For archaeologists excavating Second World War aircraft today the geology of the sites can be crucial to knowing what will have survived. Many of these aircraft had components or even major structural sections made from wood and/or covered in doped fabric: these are unlikely to have survived well in the typical burial conditions in Britain, except in some cases where deep, cold water has acted as a partial preservative. In contrast, aircraft found in the Sahara desert often have their organic components well preserved by drying. Another problem facing the archaeologists is that many of the metal components of Second World War aircraft were made of unstable aluminium alloys, particularly some with a high magnesium content that, although light, were liable to degrade into pale blue powder even when in use, and which proved vulnerable to fire and other hazards. Often these alloys made up significant amounts of the engines to save weight.

A further problem facing excavators is the hazard of unexploded ordnance (UXO). Virtually all Second World War aircraft carried machine guns for offensive or defensive use, and many carried bombs, mines or similar. Finds of ammunition are not usually dangerous in themselves, but they present legal problems for the excavators if they remove or keep the bullets, and might present a hazard to others working on or around the site subsequently. Bombs are a different matter: many German aircraft were shot down or crashed before they had released their bombs, and in many cases these had to be carefully removed from crash sites or detonated in situ. The same is true for British and American bombers, many of which crashed on take-off when heavily laden with fuel, ammunition and bombs – a particularly vulnerable point of the mission. In excavations of larger aircraft the presence of bombs is always possible, and they should be treated as live and extremely dangerous until proven otherwise or removed by military or police UXO experts.

None of these risks and problems has deterred aviation archaeologists, who in the 1960s, 1970s and 1980s excavated virtually every accessible Second World War crash site in the country – and quite a few inaccessible ones as well. Aviation archaeology emerged as a hobby in the late 1960s, particularly following the success of the film *The Battle of*

Britain. Many aviation archaeologists were children during the war and had collected shrapnel, bomb tail-fins and other remnants of the war: now they were after the big stuff.

In the early years of aviation archaeology numerous research and excavation groups were formed to excavate in different parts of the country, while many digs were also conducted by individuals or informal teams. Many of the sites were excavated with hand tools, but some teams hired mechanical diggers to reach deeper or less accessible wrecks. Some teams focused on aircraft within a defined region, while others concentrated on particular historical periods or types, such as the Battle of Britain. Early aviation archaeologists came under a great deal of criticism from archaeologists and others who felt that their methods were too crude and violent, and that their work was unscientific and told us nothing new about the history of the air war.

There certainly were cases of aviation archaeologists digging sites without due care and attention, and in some cases destroying aircraft wrecks unnecessarily to retrieve souvenirs such as instruments and control columns which they could later sell. But to apply the daintiest archaeological standards to huge aircraft already broken by a crash-landing seems absurd, particularly as the key information in an aircraft lies not in its perfectly preserved fabric but in the serial numbers and manufacturer's plates engraved, stamped or riveted onto it. Similarly, it would be ludicrous to suggest that aviation archaeology cannot tell us anything new about the history of the war. In the confusion of air combat few accurate accounts can be made of which aircraft fell where, and in the heat of the Battle of Britain and the night-raids of the Blitz, when numerous aircraft were falling to earth every night, it was impossible (and at the time largely unnecessary) to accurately record which crash site was which. Through the excavation and reporting of finds from different sites is has been possible to untangle a series of historical conundrums regarding the final resting places of various long-lost aircraft – and in many cases their crews.

The discovery of remains of aircrew in the wreckage of aircraft reflects the human tragedy of the war, and marks the sacrifice made by tens of thousands of airmen. The question of why the bodies remained in the aircraft and were not recovered is explained in more depth in a following section, but in the context of early aviation archaeology it presented a problem. Excavators finding human remains inside wrecks had been known to collect them in a carrier bag and rebury them on the same site, rather than pass them on to authorities, to avoid the legal problems that were likely to result. Today such activities are much less likely as aviation archaeologists are more aware of the legal and ethical issues around retrieving human remains. There is now a national organisation, the British Aviation Archaeology Council, which serves as a forum for different groups across the country but also provides and maintains ethical standards for excavating aircraft wrecks.

English Heritage have assessed the air crash sites of England as a part of our national heritage, and have noted that wrecked aircraft have an emotional and memorial dimension as well as a historical and archaeological one. In particular, they have noted that there were around twenty aircraft used operationally over Britain, including British, German and American types, of which there are no surviving examples left in museums or private collections. English Heritage have argued that for these 'extinct' aircraft, which include the Dornier 17 and Short Stirling bombers, the remains found from excavations of crash sites would be of particular significance as traces of otherwise vanished pieces of wartime technology.

In 1976 a team of American researchers were scanning the bottom of Loch Ness, searching for evidence of the mythical Loch Ness monster. Of Nessie they found no trace, but their sonar picked up the outline of an aircraft. On New Year's Eve 1939 a Vickers Wellington crash-landed in the loch after experiencing engine difficulty; most of the crew baled out (one dying after a parachute failure) and the pilot and co-pilot successfully ditched the aircraft and were able to deploy a life-raft before the Wellington sank to the depths of the loch. More than forty years later, a team of aviation archaeologists successfully lifted the very complete remains of the Wellington from its watery grave, using buoyant tanks and floats to bring it to the surface. The Wellington was constructed in an unusual geodetic pattern with fabric skin covering an aluminium framework; in the waters of the loch the cloth had rotted away, leaving the metal exposed. Today the Loch Ness Wellington has been restored and remains on display at the Brooklands Museum, although the restorers left the metal airframe exposed to better show its innovative, strong but labour-intensive technology.

The Naseby Hurricane

The RAF Museum in Hendon is unusual among aircraft museums in displaying several of its exhibits unrestored, in the war- and time-ravaged condition in which they were discovered. One of the most important of these is a Handley-Page Halifax, one of very few survivors of this important heavy bomber. Hendon's Halifax was recovered from the bottom of a Norwegian fjord, and on display it resembles a gigantic mastodon or dinosaur recovered from the depths: the bulky fuselage is slumped on its base, the engines have broken free of the wings and the propellers are broken, splintered wooden stumps.

Similarly evocative but a less rare specimen is the front portion and wing-stumps of a Hawker Hurricane, displayed in a diorama. No attempt has been made to restore this fragment of wreckage, which appears much as it did the day it was removed from the sand and mud of the seashore at Walton-on-the-Naze, Essex, in 1972. The story of the discovery, recovery and identification of this aircraft is one of the epic tales of aviation archaeology, told by the excavator Geoff Rayner in his excellent book *One Hurricane – One Raid*. Rayner first encountered the wreckage of the Hurricane as a schoolboy playing in the coastal marshes, when all that could be seen of the wreck was a single aluminium spar protruding from a puddle in a depression in the mud. Tentative attempts at excavation were made to identify the wreckage, but resources were scarce and the aircraft was already losing parts to other less scrupulous scavengers with hacksaws. But even from the spar the identity of the aircraft type could be deduced: four evenly spaced holes marked the locations of the Browning machine-guns that made up one-half of the armament of the Hawker Hurricane, mainstay of the RAF in the Battle of Britain and afterwards.

Years passed before Rayner was able to make a more concerted attempt to unearth the Hurricane. Digging with spade and bucket in the wet sand and cloying mud was a wearying, lonely task made more frustrating by the tendency of the pit to flood. However, at this stage a number of parts and fragments of the airframe were recovered, including part of the feed mechanisms of one of the guns, fragments of the wooden rear fuselage, and several of the aluminium panels that made up the skin of the Hurricane – several of which showed evidence of fire damage. Clues to the identity of the aircraft began to appear as well, as

Rayner trawled through the historical records and the research facility at the newly opened RAF Museum. Several false turns and misleading clues were followed before the aircraft was identified with reasonable certainty as Hurricane P3175, flown by Pilot Officer Gerard Maffett of 257 Squadron RAF, flying out of RAF Debden and its satellite airfield Martelsham Heath.

Finally the decision was made to recover the remains of the Hurricane from the unstable environment of the foreshore, where erosion threatened to wash away the mud that had protected the airframe for decades. For the last week of the dig the solitary excavation became a team effort as volunteers and local aviation enthusiasts helped to dig the airframe free from the mud and sand so that it could be winched several hundred metres to the safety of the sea wall and then recovered. By this time excavation had revealed that the aircraft lay on its back, nose slightly down, with the fuselage rear of the cockpit missing and the wings also absent apart from the stumps of spars, damaged when a wartime RAF recovery team had sawn them open to remove the machine-guns. Several panels from the aircraft's skin were recovered relatively intact, including parts of the engine cover and the area around the undercarriage. One of the heavy undercarriage legs was found almost intact, as was (more alarmingly) a considerable amount of belted .303 ammunition from one of the guns, clearly missed by the RAF in their recovery efforts.

With the help of a winch, the aircraft was dragged from its pit and rested upright on the sand, revealing parts of the cockpit remaining in the muddy wreckage, including the instrument panel and several of the instruments, the control column and the pilot's seat, the latter bent out of shape by the impact of the airframe behind. The thick laminated bullet-proof glass windscreen was discovered, shattered but intact, and was carefully recovered from the site. In the initial excavation the engine had had to be separated from the airframe as together they were too unwieldy, but the well preserved Rolls-Royce Merlin III and the remains of its propeller and reduction gears were also recovered afterwards.

The excavated remains allowed the aircraft to be positively identified as P3175, and its story emerged from historical sources. On 31 August 1940 P/O Maffett in P3175, alongside eight other Hurricanes of 257 Squadron, engaged fifty Messerschmitt 110 heavy fighters escorting a group of Dornier bombers over the Essex coast. In the engagement two

Hurricanes and one Messerschmitt were shot down; one Hurricane pilot and the Messerschmitt's crew of two were rescued from the sea. Hurricane P3175 fell rapidly, until at an altitude of around 400ft P/O Maffett managed to bale out. However, he was too low for his parachute to fully deploy, and his body was found a short distance away from the wreck of his aircraft.

Today the fragments of the Hurricane, conserved but not restored, can be seen at the RAF Museum. The story of *One Hurricane – One Raid* is one of childhood fascination inspiring an exhaustive, exhausting but ultimately successful attempt to recover and identify one of the thousands of Battle of Britain crash sites. There is no doubt that Rayner's work was archaeology of a high standard, but aviation archaeology has not always been regarded as such; Rayner describes a visit to the site by the Essex county archaeologist, charged with the management of the archaeological resource in his area. The archaeologist expressed his interest and support for the project but regretted that, being such a recent artefact, it fell outside his remit. That was 1972: today, it is hoped, a more enlightened viewpoint might prevail as professional archaeologists are increasingly recognising the capabilities of responsible amateur archaeologists in a variety of fields of study from the prehistoric to the recent past.

Excavating Paintwork: Corsair KD431

Many years ago I spent a few weeks as a volunteer helping to restore a Second World War-era North American Harvard advanced training aircraft – the type that most Spitfire and Hurricane pilots would have practised on before graduating to the real thing. The Harvard had been slightly damaged in a crash, and the repair work was used as an opportunity to carry out a more comprehensive restoration and spring-clean of the airframe and its various systems. My rather modest task was to remove the metal rods that connected the control mechanisms between the student's and instructor's cockpits, to shot-blast the old paint off them, and then to prime them and paint them afresh in a smart matt black. This immensely satisfying task saw grotty-looking components returned to their places looking factory-fresh. It never occurred to me that the many layers of paint that I was annihilating were like layers of earth on an archaeological site, each telling part of the story of the aircraft's life between its manufacture and its appearance in our work-shop.

David Morris of the Fleet Air Arm Museum in Yeovilton took a more far-sighted view in the examination of one of his aircraft, a Chance Vought Corsair built in 1944 and operated by the Fleet Air Arm before its retirement. Some mystery surrounded the aircraft, including un-certainties as to its origins, missing episodes in its history, and the rumour (later disproved) that it was the aircraft flown from Ceylon to Britain in an unorthodox return home by the remarkable Lieutenant Commander Godfrey Woodbine-Parish, commanding officer of 757 Squadron Fighter Training School. Morris, curator of aircraft at the museum, set about studying Corsair KD431 in an unprecedented level of detail: in effect he treated it as a delicate and unique archaeological site, removing layers of paint and botched repairs in a painstakingly slow process. The result of this excavation is a unique example of an un-restored Corsair in its original factory paint.

Starting at the tip of the nose and working backwards, Morris's team used scalpels, plastic scrapers, abrasives and solvents to remove the rather crude paint job applied to the aircraft when it first arrived at the museum, having previously served as a teaching aid at Cranfield College of Aeronautics. As the project progressed, clues quickly began to emerge about the aircraft's use-life: scars on the huge propeller revealed an impact with an arrester-line of the kind used to slow aircraft landing on aircraft carriers. Fragile paper labels on the engine, applied in the factory, indicated that the engine had never been removed after its first attachment. The original paintwork, scuffed and chipped on the inner-wings and around the engine, bore witness to the swarms of mechanics, armourers, pilots and others who clambered about it opening panels and loading guns during its brief period in service. Gradually old squadron markings began to appear from beneath the newer paint and the full story of KD431 could be revealed after four years of 'excavation' and research.

Corsair KD431 was an FG-1A variety, one of many built under licence by the Goodyear company in July 1944, and was given the fabri-cation number 1871 (a number found pencilled onto a component early in the project). It incorporated several prefabricated components built at other sites, some of them already in US Navy paint colours and others, built by the Brewster company, in other camouflage shades. After repainting in Royal Navy colours, it was shipped across the Atlantic: traces of the protective coatings applied for this voyage remain on the wings and engine. In 1945 KD431 was attached to 1835 Squadron before being transferred to 768 Squadron as a trainer. It was briefly mothballed before being handed over to Cranfield College of Aeronautics from where, in 1963, it came to its final home at the FAA Museum. With few surviving documents or records available from the factories, the Fleet Air Arm or the pilots who flew KD431, the majority of this story was pieced together from clues uncovered during the removal of layer after layer of paint, each revealing an earlier chapter. This archaeology of a Second World War object is one that could be replicated for any number of artefacts large and small, from weapons and uniforms to battleships, revealing hidden, forgotten or unknown aspects of their wartime lives and afterlives.

Bodies

The bullets, shells and burning fuel that tore aircraft to shreds and buried their wreckage deep in the ground wrought just as much damage on the bodies of their pilots and crews. Tens of thousands of aircrew died in the Second World War, many of them trapped in doomed aircraft or killed in explosions or by gunfire. Many others were injured, including thousands who suffered severe burns. The modern science of reconstructive surgery was founded on the work of Archibald McIndoe, a New Zealander who served as plastic surgery consultant to the RAF. McIndoe's work on reconstructing faces after severe burns, as well as the reintegration of burns victims into normal society, was honoured by his former patients who formed the 'Guinea Pig Club'. For the unlucky ones who went down with their aircraft there was the honour of a military funeral, at least for those whose aircraft had crashed on land, not into the sea. However, at many of these funerals the coffins were suspiciously light and in other cases they were weighted with sand, bricks or even potatoes to conceal an unpleasant truth: that little or nothing of the pilot had remained to be found after the crash, fire or explosion.

In many cases where aircraft crashed in Britain during the Second World War the recovery of the pilot's body was carried out by ambulance crews, coroners or the police, all accustomed to dealing with violent death. However, in cases where crash debris was scattered over a wide area or buried in the ground, the remains might not have been immediately visible, and the job of recovering them would have fallen to the RAF Maintenance Units who retrieved the fragments of airframe. Often, particularly at the height of the Battle of Britain, these recovery duties were subcontracted to construction or removal firms who would also have been responsible for collecting human remains. In the aftermath of a violent crash, explosion or petrol fire it was frequently impossible to recover more than a few shreds of tissue, and in aircraft with more than one crew-member the remains were often so mixed up that they could not be distinguished. Military regulations decreed that to ascertain death from body fragments required a total of 7lb of tissue, or any single fragment of skull or spine, without which life was highly unlikely to have been sustained. In some cases partial or badly burnt bodies could be recovered, in others a few parts, and in many cases nothing at all. However, there were also bodies that could not be retrieved – those that had remained in their aircraft and been driven deep into the ground. Under wartime conditions it was often impossible to recover these with the tools available, and resources were better used retrieving aircraft that could be made airworthy again. Records of casualty recovery from these sites were often incomplete, lost or falsified to spare the feelings of the relatives – after all, a funeral even with an empty or mostly empty coffin still offered a chance for relatives to mourn, provided they did not know what the coffin contained. Among servicemen the weighted coffins were an open secret, as anyone who had seen an air-crash might have suspected. There are reports that several sets of incomplete human remains were buried in tin boxes on the site of an air-base hospital in Leicestershire; the bodies were recovered after the empty coffins had already been dispatched for burial, and remain on the site to this day.

Problems began to emerge with the rise of aviation archaeology from the 1960s onwards, as increasing numbers of inaccessible aircraft were being excavated, some of which still contained human remains, even if just a few fragments of bone. While some aviation archaeologists reported all finds of human remains to the coroner or the RAF, others were less scrupulous, and some excavators found that earlier diggers had already pillaged crash sites for souvenirs and left the remains of the pilot behind. In 1986 the Protection of Military Remains Act (PMRA) came into force, making it a crime to excavate or interfere with a military shipwreck or air crash site in Britain, if it was known or suspected to contain human remains. Aviation archaeologists were required to apply for licences to excavate RAF crash sites, and only those sites that were recorded as having no human remains were licensed. However, given the lack of accuracy in the wartime records and the 'white lie' of a coffin full of bricks, it was inevitable that the remains of RAF aircrew would begin to be found where none was supposed to be.

Sergeant Dennis Noble

In 1996 a team of aviation archaeologists began an excavation near a street corner in Hove, East Sussex. Their aim was to recover the remains of Hawker Hurricane P3179, a close relation of P3175 recovered from Walton-on-the-Naze (see above). From the first few inches of soil it was clear that the excavators were in luck: fragments of the propeller and other components were visible in the earth and soon large parts of the airframe were revealed. But as the forward fuselage of the Hurricane came into view, it became apparent that the pilot's body was still in the wreckage. In accordance with the law, the excavators stopped work and informed the police, and the coroner removed the body of Sergeant Dennis Noble, who had been killed in action in August 1940 aged just 20 years old.

Noble, an electrical engineer, had joined the RAF Volunteer Reserve in 1938 and trained as a pilot. From September 1939 his training was brought forward and in 1940 he was posted to an Operational Training Unit for 11 Group of Fighter Command, learning to fly the Hawker Hurricane. Later that year he joined 43 Squadron at RAF Tangmere, and on 16 August, just two weeks before his death, he shot down a Junkers 87 dive-bomber during an attack on Tangmere.

On the morning of 30 August Noble and 43 Squadron attacked a formation of Junkers 88 bombers and Messerschmitt 109 fighters over Hove. During the engagement Hurricane P3179 was seen to fall out of formation and crash into a street in the town. The aircraft formed a crater that filled with water from a broken pipe, and burning fuel set fires in nearby buildings. The wings and tail of the Hurricane remained broken on the ground, but the heavy engine had driven the cockpit and forward fuselage deep into the ground. The salvage crew who removed the surviving components of the aircraft claimed that they had also recovered the remains of Sergeant Noble, who was buried with full military honours near his family home in Nottinghamshire a few days later. At the funeral the coffin appeared suspiciously light to some, and the first hints emerged that perhaps the body had not been recovered from its battlefield grave.

In 1995 the Southern Counties Aviation Club sought permission to excavate the site, and as it was not recorded as a war grave the licence was granted. In November 1996 the excavation went ahead. The first sign that Sergeant Noble might not have been recovered was the presence of his parachute which had two blood-stained bullet holes in it. Below the parachute the first human remains were discovered. With official permission the team continued to recover the remains, which the excavators estimated were at least 80 per cent complete, and included some of Noble's personal effects, such as his wallet. It was clear to the archaeologists that few or none of the remains could have been recovered in 1940. The findings sparked anger and grief among the Noble family, who demanded an explanation from the RAF. Following an inquest, Dennis Noble's remains were buried in his original grave, and the new building next to the crash site in Hove was named Noble Court in his honour.

Summary

Like so many aspects of the Second World War, the air battles over Britain are approaching the edge of living memory. As the pilots that flew the aircraft and the servicemen and women who kept them flying grow older, leaving fewer and fewer surviving, a greater burden of commemoration will fall on the remains that they left behind. Across the country the remnants of airfields, aircraft and a few of the aircrew remain buried beneath the earth or lost and forgotten. At the same time valiant efforts are being made by volunteers and enthusiasts to keep at least some of the airfields open as museums, and to keep a growing number of wartime aircraft in the air. For those that are lost, there are teams of dedicated local historians and aviation archaeologists searching out and recording the smallest traces that remain. The chances of reuniting retired RAF pilots with the newly discovered wreckage of their wartime aircraft grow smaller every day, but the enduring popular fascination with the Second World War in the air will ensure that their legacy is preserved and honoured long after they are gone.

Further Reading

Arnold, Keith, *Green Two: Sgt Dennis Noble, one of Churchill's Few 1940* (Southern Counties Aviation Research, 2003)

de la Bédoyère, Guy, *Battles Over Britain: the Archaeology of the Air War* (Tempus, 2000)

de la Bédoyère, Guy, *Aviation Archaeology in Britain* (Shire, 2001)

Buchan Innes, Graham, *British Airfield Buildings of the Second World War* (Midland Publishing, 1997)

Capdevila, Luc and Daniele Voldman, *War Dead: Western Societies and the Casualties of War* (Edinburgh University Press, 2006)

Clarke, Bob, *The Archaeology of Airfields* (History Press, 2007)

English Heritage, *Military Aircraft Crash Sites: Archaeological Guidance on their Significance and Future Management* (English Heritage, 2002)

Freeman, Roger, *Bases of Bomber Command, Then and Now* (After the Battle, 2001)

Lindqvist, Sven, *A History of Bombing* (Granta, 2002)

McLachlan, Ian, *Final Flights: Dramatic Wartime Incidents Revealed by Aviation Archaeology* (Patrick Stephens, 1994)

Morris, David, *The Time Capsule Fighter: Corsair KD431* (Sutton, 2006)

Overy, Richard, *The Air War 1939–1945* (Stein & Day, 1980)

Raynor, Geoff, *One Hurricane – One Raid* (Airlife, 1990)

Robertson, Bruce, *Aviation Archaeology: a Collector's Guide to Aeronautical Relics* (Patrick Stephens, 1977)

Sarkar, Dilip, *Missing in Action: Resting in Peace?* (Ramrod Publications, 2006)

Saunders, Andy, *Finding the Few: Some Outstanding Mysteries of the Battle of Britain Investigated and Solved* (Grub Street, 2009)

Saunders, Andy, *Finding the Foe: Outstanding Luftwaffe Mysteries of the Battle of Britain and Beyond Investigated and Solved* (Grub Street, 2010)

Wells, Mark, *Courage and Air Warfare: the Allied Aircrew Experience in the Second World War* (Frank Cass, 1995)

Useful Websites

www.rafbombercommand.com

This site is devoted to the history of Bomber Command in the Second World War. It includes technical information, historical data, stories and more. The site is linked to the Bomber Command Association, an ex-service group.

www.battleofbritain1940.net

The website of the Battle of Britain Historical Society, containing a great deal of information on the history, heritage and memorials of the battle.

www.aviationarchaeology.org.uk

This is the official site of the British Aviation Archaeology Council, a membership organisation that upholds ethical standards in aviation archaeology as well as providing research resources and publishing a newsletter.

www.airfieldresearchgroup.org.uk

The Airfield Research Group studies the history of civilian and military airfields in Britain. The website contains articles, links to publications and reports and information for members.

Places to Visit

Imperial War Museum Duxford

This former First and Second World War airfield now houses one of the world's greatest collections of vintage aircraft. Used by the British and American air forces in the Second World War, it was for a time the home base of fighter ace Douglas Bader. Its collection includes iconic Second World War aircraft including Spitfires and a Lancaster, as well as a number of privately owned airworthy aircraft housed at the museum. Every year Duxford hosts a number of air shows, where flying Second World War aircraft operated by the RAF's Battle of Britain Memorial Flight and others can be seen.

IWM Duxford
Cambridge

CB22 4QR
www.iwm.org.uk/visits/iwm-duxford

Royal Air Force Museum London

The RAF Museum is in two parts, one in north London and one in Cosford near Birmingham. The London branch is based at the historic Hendon Aerodrome, and houses a research library and archive as well as an impressive collection of aircraft. Among its collection of Second World War aircraft are rare surviving examples of some German aircraft including a Messerschmitt 110 and a radar-equipped Junkers 88. Free admission.

RAF Museum London
Grahame Park Way
London
NW9 5LL
www.rafmuseum.org.uk/london/

Royal Air Force Museum Cosford

Like the London branch of the museum, RAF Museum Cosford houses a large number of rare and historically important aircraft, many of them dating from the Second World War, including a Mosquito, a Hurricane, a Catalina flying boat, and rare German Messerschmitt 410 and Messerschmitt 163 rocket-powered interceptors. Free admission.

RAF Museum Cosford
Shifnal
Shropshire
TF11 8UP
www.rafmuseum.org.uk/cosford/

Chapter 6

The Air Raid Warden

In 1928 schoolteacher E. Ite Ekpenyon travelled from his native Nigeria to London to study law. Financial difficulties hampered his studies and in September 1939, at the outbreak of war, he was still in London, so he enrolled as an air raid warden in Marylebone. In an account of his war work broadcast on the BBC Empire Service, he described his training and experiences as a warden and later as a senior warden and deputy post warden. The very common nature of Ekpenyon's experiences alongside his outsider's perspective on Britain at war makes his account of warden training and warden work all the more interesting, throwing light on this often forgotten aspect of war work – one that was experienced by more than a million people in the course of the conflict, and which left its traces in the form of wardens' posts, air raid shelters and other more portable or ephemeral traces such as warning notices, badges and uniforms, bells and whistles.

In the phoney war period before the bombs began to fall on cities, the air raid wardens were trained in all aspects of their likely work. Ekpenyon describes the process of registering as a warden and being allocated a patrol area near his home, and the lecture series he attended that covered subjects ranging from first aid and protection against poison gas, to incendiary bomb disposal and the role of the warden in relation to the public and the civil defence authorities. In addition to their training, wardens were expected to be able to speak on these subjects to a public audience, passing on the lessons about gas protection and the importance of maintaining the blackout – a forum in which Ekpenyon's background in teaching no doubt stood him in good stead. Wardens were recruited to work in the areas where they lived, and their knowledge of the community – augmented by censuses of households – was a major asset in their work: a warden would know how many people were resident in a particular bombed house so that rescuers could stop or continue their searches as necessary.

Once the bombing began, a great deal of the warden's work was devoted to the management of air raid shelters: ensuring that they were opened in advance of the raid and that they were clean, orderly and properly equipped. During air raids one of the warden's duties – and one that Ekpenyon seems to have excelled at – was to do the rounds of public shelters and maintain morale and calm. One of the problems that he encountered in the larger public shelters was a racist mob mentality focused on minorities and refugees, a mood that often threatened to spill over into violence. The threat of race riots was a constant one during the Blitz and one that many histories of the war have tended to ignore. As an African with authority in the shelters, Ekpenyon was able to defuse ethnic tensions and maintain order with the help of shelter marshals. In many shelters a community atmosphere prevailed, and Ekpenyon describes Christmas parties and tea parties in some of the shelters in his patrol area.

Due to their ages and reserved occupations, none of my immediate family served in the armed forces during the Second World War, but my great-grandfather was an air raid warden and our family collection of wartime memorabilia includes his uniform insignia. These consist of embroidered shoulder badges marked 'warden' and a brass badge bearing the ARP insignia – common souvenirs of wartime service in civil defence, and a surviving trace of a service that can claim to be the largest organised civilian force in wartime Britain. In this chapter I will outline the archaeological remains of wartime air raid precautions, focusing in particular on the most abundant of all wartime survivors: the air raid shelters that lie in, on or beneath our lawns, parks, playing fields and basements.

Air Raid Precautions

From the early 1920s it was widely recognised that any future war was likely to include a potentially devastating aerial bombing campaign, and a programme of air raid precautions (ARP) was put in place under the auspices of the Home Office. The activities of this department ranged from coordinating the design and manufacture of gas masks to the stockpiling of coffins to hold the anticipated mass casualties. From 1934 the ARP committee had been examining the possibility of forming a civilian air raid wardens' service, based on an existing model in Germany, and had even considered making them part of the police force. In March 1937 the formation of the air raid wardens' service was announced in Parliament, with their stated role being liaison between the civil defence authorities and the public. Members of the public were invited to volunteer for this service, and the Home Office emphasised their preference for responsible individuals of good standing in their local area, who (alongside their various roles of reporting and managing bomb sites and other incidents) were to set an example of steadfastness to the wider population. Wardens were to operate from fixed posts in groups of two or three, each responsible for a sector of several hundred people. As part of the planning for civil defence, each local authority was supposed to identify buildings suitable for use as wardens' posts and first aid posts, as well as for local ARP command centres and gas mask storage depots. In many cases wardens' posts were their own homes or empty shops, but in places where no suitable buildings were available wardens' posts were constructed, many of them in the form of concrete pillboxes or smaller versions of the brick-built surface air raid shelter described below. Government grants were available for their construction by local authorities, and they were designed to be blast- and shrapnel-proof yet easy for the public to identify and locate during incidents. Their principal function was to provide a hub for organisation and communication, with telephone connections to the nearest ARP control centre and equipment including whistles and bells, first aid kits, torches, fire-fighting equipment and protective clothing. Given their small size – some were compared to protected telephone kiosks – they were not designed to provide protection for more than one or two wardens, often in sectors where much larger teams were located. In many cases these purpose-built wardens' posts were demolished at the end of the war, like most street air raid shelters, but a few have survived, although attempts to monitor them suggest that many have been demolished in recent years, probably due to a lack of awareness or understanding of their role and heritage value.

The Wardens' Service

From the foundation of the wardens' service to the end of the war around 1.4 million people, one in six of them women, served as air raid wardens in some capacity. Over the years the form and function of the wardens' service varied, as did their training and even their uniform. In the early days of the service wardens were expected to wear their own clothes, supplemented by an armband and a metal helmet painted black with a white 'W'. Later many wardens were given navy blue overalls and wellington boots, and in 1941 proper uniforms in dark blue serge were issued to all. Many wardens carried a more advanced respirator than the general public, designed to provide longer-lasting protection in contaminated areas. Many were also equipped with heavy oilcloth anti-gas outfits for decontamination work.

Air raid wardens were given extensive training in a bewildering variety of subjects and skills so that they could deal with any of the numerous threats and situations the war was expected to throw up. Some of these skills, such as the safe disposal of incendiary bombs, proved to be highly relevant and were frequently put into practice; others, such as assisting in gas decontamination, never emerged in real life. While serious fires caused by bombing were the responsibility of the fire services, wardens were expected to be able to tackle small fires, and were equipped with stirrup pumps, short hoses, buckets and sandbags for this purpose. Similarly, the wardens were expected to carry out first-aid on minor casualties, while more serious cases were the responsibility of the ambulance services. In fire-fighting, first-aid and other areas such as policing incident sites and rescuing survivors from collapsed buildings, air raid wardens were expected to take on the roles of all of the standard and some of the wartime emergency services – a heavy burden for the largely volunteer force.

In peacetime and in the early months of the war the warden's roles were fairly routine and were widely regarded as intrusive and rather officious. Wardens patrolled the streets during the night making sure that the blackout was maintained, and became known for shouting 'cover that window' or 'put that light out'. They also provided training in the fitting and correct use of gas masks and other protective equipment, as well as gas-proofing rooms and equipping refuge rooms. In all of these roles the air raid wardens, in the months before the bombing of cities began in earnest, functioned and were regarded as the eyes and arms of the Home Office with regard to air raid precautions and the public. Up to the outbreak of war their training and preparation were at best patchy: at the time of the Munich Crisis in 1938 many air raid wardens had yet to receive any protective or identifying equipment, with a particular shortage of the steel helmets vital for safety in an air raid. The increase in membership numbers to over a million shortly afterwards did little to aid the situation.

It was not until the bombs began to fall in earnest that the true value of the air raid wardens became clear. Under the bombs the months or years of training were put to good effect and the wardens came to be regarded by the public as an essential wartime emergency service. Wardens were usually the first on the scene following a bombing, dispatching runners with messages to the local command centre and managing services at the scene. As first responders the wardens were faced with a variety of hazards: still-burning incendiary bombs had to be extinguished with sandbags or buckets of sand; burnt or broken buildings threatened to collapse even as casualties remained trapped in the wreckage; unexploded bombs lurked in craters and there was the ever-present threat of a second wave of bombers. Within minutes fire crews, rescue squads and ambulances would attend, but until their arrival the air raid warden's duties covered all of theirs: they shepherded shocked survivors to rest centres or shelters, provided first-aid as required, and attempted to extricate people trapped or wounded in the ruins of their homes. Once the emergency services had arrived, the role of the warden became a supervisory or coordinating one, directing the operations of the rescue squads and fire crews based on their knowledge of the area and its population. The work of the air raid wardens was physically and emotionally exhausting, as well as dangerous: hundreds of wardens were killed on duty and many thousands more were injured in the course of the war. In Bromley, South London, there is a memorial to two air raid wardens who were killed by a bomb while on duty. Gladys Muriel Blinkhorn-Hay and Leslie Frederick Hurst died when their wardens' post in St Mark's School was destroyed by a direct hit in December 1940. The site was purchased and planted as a memorial by the local council. For their bravery in rescuing people trapped in bombsites, and for continuing to work in the face of extreme risks, a number of wardens across the country were awarded medals, including the George Cross. With well over a million members, the air raid wardens' service was probably the largest single service, military or civilian, in wartime Britain. The wardens, most of them volunteers, made a considerable contribution to the population's overall resilience in the face of the bombs. As respected members of the community they were able, wherever possible, to maintain calm in the face of the horrors of war and to largely (although not completely) stave off the dangerous panic that gripped civilian populations across the world in wartime as cities burned around them.

The Heritage of Air Raid Precautions

Air raid precautions touched the lives of every person in Britain during the Second World War, and in its material forms it impinged on numerous aspects of everyday life, from the ubiquitous gas mask to the thick blackout curtains on every window, the steel helmet on the hat-stand and the air raid shelter in the garden. It is not surprising that so many of these objects and sites have survived in considerable numbers across the country, but sadly the vast majority have been lost, often very recently, as few recognise their historical importance or even, in many cases, understand what they are. Nonetheless in gardens, cellars and attics, and even at the back of old wardrobes, there lurk the remnants of the biggest campaign of civil defence in the nation's history. On moving into a new house several years ago I explored the darker corners of the attic and found an old trunk that contained, among many old and spider-infested blankets, two air raid warden steel helmets. One of these was a standard Mark 2 helmet of the kind used by British troops throughout the war, painted black. The other was a smaller helmet with a higher dome: a Zuckerman helmet, named after the senior government scientist Solly Zuckerman who designed it. It was created specifically for civil defence work, where hazards were much more likely to be falling objects – shrapnel, building materials and so on – than projectiles such as bullets. These helmets were issued to civil defence staff including air raid wardens, and were also made available for private purchase. These Second World War relics were hidden in an utterly typical 1930s suburban semi – who knows how many other civil defence artefacts are yet to be found across the country?

Air Raid Shelters

Perhaps the most common of all home front heritage sites, as well as being one of the most neglected, is the air raid shelter: probably Britain's greatest untapped resource of Second World War archaeology. In parks and back gardens, in homes, workplaces and public buildings there are shelters or the traces of shelters bearing witness to the fear and reality of German bombs. These curious and gloomy structures have often been reused as sheds or storage spaces, while many have rotted away or been demolished. Some were sealed in 1945 in anticipation of future wars that never came. These shelters, particularly the public shelters buried beneath parks and school playing fields, serve as time capsules of the war years for the archaeologists who are beginning to open them up. Opening an air raid shelter is the closest most British archaeologists can get to uncovering an ancient tomb: breaking in, shining a torch and announcing that they can see 'Things! Wonderful things!' While the rusty fittings, mouldy benches, musty sandbags and traces of graffiti found in the shelters are hardly the treasures of Tutankhamen, they offer archaeologists a glimpse of civilian life in wartime Britain that, like so many aspects of the war, is nearing the edge of living memory. To preserve and record these memories we need to protect their material traces, and this is the task that heritage enthusiasts and professionals have set themselves in exploring Britain's surviving air raid shelters.

To understand the shelters we need to understand their history. In Britain this stretches back to the early years of the First World War, when German Zeppelins first began their attacks on cities, and stretches through the 1920s and 1930s to the harsh lessons learnt from Barcelona's experiences of bombing during the Spanish Civil War. The history of air raid precautions in Britain is also a decidedly political one, with vigorous campaigns by the Communist Party, led by figures such as J.B.S. Haldane, for better shelters in working class areas in the face of Home Office dithering. The history of air raid shelters also explains the bewildering variety of forms that survive today, with the smallest holding one or two people and the largest several thousand.

Britain's oldest surviving air raid shelter is in Cleethorpes, Lincolnshire. Now a rather nondescript garage with thick concrete walls and ceiling, in 1916 it was built for local businessman Joseph Forrester after Zeppelin bombs killed thirty-one soldiers billeted nearby. The first bomb dropped on Britain by a German aircraft had fallen on Christmas Eve 1914, breaking windows around Dover Castle, and from 1915 raids by Zeppelins of the German army and navy rained down high-explosive bombs on towns and cities including Edinburgh, London, Kings Lynn, Sunderland and Yarmouth. Later in the war heavier-than-air craft such as the Gotha bomber continued to terrorise populations across the country, with Londoners taking shelter in Underground stations in an eerie premonition of the Blitz. While some air raid shelters were privately built during the First World War the idea of dedicated refuges came later, as the developments of bomber technology through the 1920s and 1930s began to convince politicians and military planners that future wars would be won and lost in the air above enemy cities. Stanley Baldwin MP famously declared that 'the bomber will always get through' and, with bombs or poison gas, lay waste to urban areas; the only remedy, he argued, was to be prepared to do the same in return.

In the face of an apparently unstoppable bomber threat there were few advances in air raid shelter technology until the second half of the 1930s, when the Spanish Civil War, and later the Munich Crisis, convinced British politicians that an air war was approaching against which the population must – and could – be protected. While the bombing of Guernica, so dramatically rendered by Picasso, has lingered in historical accounts, it was the bombing of Barcelona, a modern European city, that most horrified and fascinated observers of the fascist insurgency in Spain. Italian aircraft flying from Majorca flew hundreds of raids against the city, while the people of Barcelona took shelter in tunnels dug beneath the city by community groups and volunteers organised by citizen councils. Foreign scientists eager to improve the air raid protection in their home countries studied these innovative shelters, along with the damage wrought by modern bombs. From Britain the Labour Party sent civil engineer Cyril Helsby to review the effects of bombs on modern buildings, while the Communist Party dispatched the scientist J.B.S. Haldane, co-inventor with his father of the British army's gas masks during the First World War. Today archaeologists in Barcelona are beginning to uncover some of the forgotten miles of tunnels dug under the city, many of which were sealed at the war's end in 1939, with 'modern' fittings including plumbing, ventilation and electric lighting still in place.

In Britain the responsibility for air raid protection was given to local councils, initially at least without any funds being allocated. Some councils took the initiative in planning for air raid shelters and the associated infrastructure of auxiliary fire stations, gas decontamination centres and warden posts. Other councils delayed acting on the guidelines for too long, and many restricted their activities to digging trenches in parks and public spaces. These meagre and miserable holes in the ground, reminiscent of First World War trenches, offered moderate protection from bombs but none from the elements, and most became flooded or clogged with refuse. Meanwhile private contractors began to offer bespoke air raid shelters for homes and workplaces with varying degrees of luxury and safety, including air conditioning and gas-proof doors. The prevalence of privately built shelters explains the remarkable diversity in Britain's air raid shelter heritage – unlike pillboxes and military installations, there were no standard designs, so local practices together with raw material shortages have produced a high degree of variation that archaeologists are only now beginning to record.

Sheltering at Home

Given the government's reluctance to fund large public shelters in virtually all parts of the country, it was natural that civil defence would largely concentrate on protecting the population within their own homes. Initially there was a focus on the gas threat, and householders were instructed to prepare one of the rooms in the house – preferably the bathroom – as an airtight gas-proof refuge. This proved both practically unfeasible and ill advised, as it was soon realised that any gas bombing was likely to be accompanied by conventional bombing. In the months leading up to the outbreak of war, preparing homes for protection against bombs took two forms: the construction of shelters in back gardens and the reinforcement of cellars, basements or under-stair cupboards. The latter involved the installation of wooden or steel joists and supports to create a space that could physically withstand the collapse of the house on top of it. Most of these structures offered no protection against a direct hit from even the smallest bombs, but they did provide shelter from the statistically far more likely collapse or partial collapse of buildings caused by the shockwaves from bombs detonating underground. While most of the reinforcing materials were removed from homes in the aftermath of the war, as they were bulky and often made access to basements difficult, many homes around the country still retain the wooden beams and steel fittings that promised to protect against the German air force.

Back garden air raid shelters fall into roughly two categories: the vast majority, more than 2.5 million, were Anderson shelters, while the remainder were a mixture of bespoke or modular shelters purchased by the homeowners and installed by building contractors. The iconic Anderson shelters, named after Home Secretary Sir John Anderson, were designed by the engineer William Patterson and distributed freely, or sold cheaply, to households with gardens. The Anderson was a small, curve-topped structure measuring approximately 2 metres by 1.4 metres, and constructed from sheets of corrugated steel. To assemble the Anderson a hole was dug to a depth of around a metre, and the shelter was assembled inside the hole with a step or two down into the raised entrance. The earth from the digging was then piled up on top of the shelter to a recommended height of 18 inches; many people planted grass or vegetables on the tops of their Andersons. Inside the shelter there were seats or bunks for four to six people. Built of thin metal without a door, floor, drainage or ventilation, most Andersons were cold, damp and prone to flooding, but they offered a reasonable level of protection from anything short of a direct hit. Some owners adapted their shelters to make them more comfortable, adding wooden floors, drainage sumps, lighting and a door; others painted the exposed front panels of the shelters to resemble cottages or play-houses. Due to their construction from thin metal the Anderson was prone to rust and large numbers have not survived into the present. Even the ones I recall seeing in gardens twenty years ago are disappearing at a rapid rate as a rusting shelter quickly becomes a waterlogged health hazard of interest only to rats, foxes and archaeologists. However, an archaeological survey of Anderson shelters in Southampton has indicated that their survival rate might be better than expected. Around 12 per cent of homes surveyed had either surviving Andersons or at least the traces or remains of shelters. This research suggests that across the country there are the surviving remains of hundreds of thousands of Anderson shelters, probably the biggest and most accessible Second World War archaeological resource that remains, and one that has only just begun to be studied.

Before the first of the millions of Andersons had been manufactured and installed, many homeowners had made their own arrangements to protect themselves and their families from bombs. In magazines and newspapers from the late 1930s there are advertisements for air raid shelters that look considerably more luxurious than Andersons, with solid-looking airtight doors, lighting and proper bunks and seats. In Shooters Hill, south London, archaeologist Andy Brockman has explored some of the privately built shelters in this middle-class residential area, including brick-built blast shelters in back gardens that were installed at a cost of £30. In one of the gardens he found a substantial air raid shelter in the form of an underground concrete bunker hidden under a rockery. This bunker, which straddled two gardens and had entrances from both, included two rooms, lighting, power, drainage and an escape shaft. The shelter had been built by the Cuffley and Griffiths families, neighbours who shared the cost of construction of what must have been one of the most comfortable and secure private shelters in any British back garden. While the Cuffley and Griffiths shelter was built to a specific order, many more reasonably well-off households installed shelters marketed by enterprising construction firms in the run-up to war.

In Edgware, north London, I was invited to survey the possible remains of a shelter beneath a flowerbed in a private garden. A previous owner of the house had visited and expressed an interest in seeing the shelter, which the current owners had been unaware of. My inspection of the flowerbed revealed the fragmented remains of a large concrete Stanton shelter, built out of steel-reinforced concrete segments delivered to the site and installed in a pre-excavated hole. Further investigation of the flowerbed uncovered the remains of an entrance stairway, which revealed brick interior walls dividing the main part of the shelter and the entranceway, presumably for the comfort of those inside. The Stanton company manufactured shelters for civilian and military customers, at one point turning out sections at a rate equivalent to one complete shelter per hour. According to the woman who remembered living in the house in wartime, this shelter, installed by a crew from her father's construction firm, had been built too close to the water-table so that the first time it was used it was found to be ankle-deep in water, and the family decided to take their chances in the house, sleeping in the garage during air raids. At some point after the war the shelter had been broken up and filled in: only the ends of some of the sections remained sticking out of the soil like broken ribs, although the staircase appeared to have been left in situ, perhaps as it was made of one solid and substantial lump of concrete. Further investigation of this site is planned but, as the shelter was never used by the family who owned it, an excavation would reveal little if anything about the people but might tell us more about how the shelter was constructed.

Sheltering in Public

As there was no guarantee that people would be at home when an air raid began, local councils were supposed to provide additional protection in the form of public air raid shelters in streets, squares, parks and other public places, sufficient for 10 per cent of the population. Many councils struggled to meet this requirement: some designated vacant shops as public shelters, while others merely dug holes in public land. Most public shelters dug in parks and waste ground were trench shelters, often little more than holes in the ground with staircases leading down into them. Based on the trenches of the First World War, these would have been reasonably effective against bomb fragments and flying splinters but little use against falling masonry and direct hits. In addition, they were not designed for long-term use, and once it became clear that night-bombing meant that the population would often have to sleep in shelters, they were mostly either abandoned or upgraded, bringing them into line with other trench shelters that were lined with wood, brick, corrugated iron or concrete, and covered with a roof of concrete or steel with a layer of earth to absorb blast.

Trench shelters built to government standards were designed to hold fifty people, with bench seats installed and at least one chemical toilet or bucket in a cubicle. Most had two access points: a staircase for general use, usually at right angles to the interior to protect from bomb blasts, and an emergency exit at the far end to use in case the staircase was blocked with fallen masonry. Due to their construction methods, size and subterranean nature, trench shelters are some of the most common surviving shelters in Britain, although they are often hidden and forgotten. Some trench shelters were dug more shallowly into the ground, and their earth-covered roofs raised above the surface to form a long, low mound. These 'semi-sunken' shelters are easier to spot on the surface, and often have an oval or circular cross-section. Some were made from large sections of concrete pipe. The most common types of semi-sunken shelter were the Stanton shelters described above, with curved roofs of reinforced concrete built in modular form so that they could be delivered and installed to order in a range of sizes.

A few years ago, while excavating a Victorian rubbish dump on the edge of a park in Hendon, north London, I spotted an odd concrete 'mushroom' on the side of a slope in the park. Closer examination revealed this to be one of five such mushrooms, about a metre across and half a metre high, spread in a line up the side of a hill. Each of these was the emergency exit shaft of a trench shelter, and the mushroom-tops proved to be heavy concrete plugs placed on the exit hatches in 1945 to seal them closed. Approximately 20 metres along from each of the exits, I found flat slabs resembling graves; these were the entrance staircases of the five shelters, sealed (as I discovered by inspecting them from inside) by a layer of corrugated iron and a six-inch layer of concrete. In order to examine the shelters, we decided to open two of them: one by excavating the earth and rubble (and wild horseradish) that filled its staircase, the other by chiselling away the concrete that sealed its exit shaft. Both proved to be long, slow and difficult jobs: the first plagued by the horseradish that made our eyes water, the second because concrete is strong stuff. Eventually we were able to climb inside the shelters and look around. Both were built to the same design, as expected: a standard fifty-person trench shelter approximately 17 metres long, with toilet cubicles at each end and a drainage sump below the iron ladder to the emergency exit, sealed with a heavy steel door below the concrete. The shelters were built from shuttered concrete cast in place, and traces of wooden shuttering could be seen on the walls and ceiling. They had clearly been equipped with electric lights and ventilation: a heavy insulated cable appeared through the side walls and connected to a Bakelite fixture attached to the side of one of the toilet cubicles. Our survey of the shelters included careful measurements of every dimension and a record of the objects that had been left inside them – mostly 1940s rubbish thrown in shortly before they were sealed. On one of the walls we found a trace of words on the concrete: 'A. FAIRGRIEVE ADAMS . . . Medical Officer . . .'

A search of the records of the borough council, carried out alongside the excavation, revealed that Alfred Fairgrieve Adamson had been medical officer of health for the borough of Hendon for many years, including throughout the Second World War. He retired in 1954 and died in 1976 at the age of 86. With better lighting, it became clear that the fragment of text was part of a poster that had been glued to the wall of the shelter, one of several whose traces could be seen on the walls, but only in this one part had the text been transferred from the paper to the concrete. Presumably the poster would have been some sort of warning about public health in the shelter – a reminder that 'coughs and sneezes spread diseases' or similar. The two shelters in Sunny Hill Park were surveyed and found to be in remarkably good condition, although one had cracked slightly due to subsidence in the hillside. This shelter was resealed by filling the entrance staircase with rubble and earth, while the second shelter was sealed with a locked steel hatch to enable future entry.

Subterranea Britannica

The excavation, survey and recording of the shelters in Hendon was assisted by members of the underground study group Subterranea Britannica, a society for people with an interest in manmade underground spaces in Britain (and beyond), including mines, bunkers, tunnels and sewers. Members of the society visit these sites, often with special permission, and record them through photography, surveying and drawing. Sub Brit, as the group is more commonly known, produces a magazine, *Subterranea*, which contains a great deal of interesting historical and archaeological information about air raid shelters and related subjects. While they have recorded some small shelters, some of Sub Brit's most important contributions to the archaeology of air raid shelters relate to large and complex tunnel systems that were built or adapted to provide public refuges in various parts of the country.

Deep Shelters

The use of London Underground stations as shelters in the First World War, together with the insights from Barcelona, led many in 1930s Britain to advocate the construction of deep bomb-proof shelters. These were supposed to provide large numbers of people with complete protection either deep underground or under metres of concrete (or both). Due to their depth, solid construction and capacity for reuse, most of the relatively small number of Second World War deep shelters have survived, often serving as archives or storage spaces. The deep shelters built as extensions of several London Underground stations are some of the best known survivors, and many have been recorded and photographed by Subterranea Britannica. Deep air raid shelters inspired what is probably one of the rudest songs of the Second World War, *The Deepest Shelter in Town*, in which a lady implores her lover to stay with her and explore said site of refuge. Some of the largest deep shelters, in the form of tunnel systems dug into cliffs and below towns, held tens of thousands of people in relative comfort. Due to their size, deep shelters often contained better facilities, including clinics and ventilation.

The Ramsgate Tunnels comprise a network stretching for around 4 miles beneath the town and incorporating existing railway tunnels. The tunnels were dug into the chalk underlying the Kent town, which was soft enough to mine easily but strong enough not to need propping or lining in most places. Once dug, they were fitted with seating, lights, toilets, ventilation shafts, a tannoy system and first aid posts. The total cost of the project exceeded £50,000 but it offered deep, bomb-proof shelter for around 35,000 people, making it surprisingly cost-effective for the local council. Sub Brit have surveyed the Ramsgate Tunnels twice, in 1984 and in 1997. Photographs from the war years show benches and electric lighting in the tunnels, which in their layout, cross-section and fittings very closely resemble the shelters built in Barcelona just a few years before. This suggests that the borough engineer R.D. Brimmell, who designed the scheme, was, in the parlance of the time, 'Barcelona-minded' or aware of the real threats that civilian populations faced from bombing.

Today the Ramsgate Tunnels are largely forgotten, despite occasional plans to turn them into a heritage visitor attraction, and most of the multiple entrance points are sealed up. However, survey work by Sub Brit has shown that in many places original wartime fittings, notices and infrastructure survive in situ, as well as the miles of tunnels themselves, dug in 1939 to Brimmell's plan. Sub Brit have also drawn attention to the condition of parts of the tunnel, some of which have collapsed or appear likely to collapse. Other more accessible areas have been vandalised over the years, and a great deal of the original infrastructure has been lost or destroyed. Surveys such as this are a central part of studying Second World War archaeological heritage, as they enable us to highlight the threats and neglect that it faces and to prioritise conservation and restoration efforts.

Between 1938 and 1939 a series of tunnels were dug into the sandstone beneath Stockport, Greater Manchester. Like the tunnels beneath Ramsgate, these deep shelters were designed to provide a high level of protection for thousands of people. The tunnels were laid out in grids, with long galleries fitted with benches and three-tier bunk beds for overnight stays. Electricity was installed and toilets built in to maintain hygiene in the shelters – a serious concern at the time. The largest of the shelters held up to 6,500 people and the smallest more than 2,000. By the end of the war the shelters had largely fallen out of use, and they were sealed up for possible future reuse.

Today the largest of these complexes forms the basis of the Stockport Air Raid Shelters, a unique museum showing what life was like beneath the streets of the town during air raids. The museum is largely aimed at school parties, and provides an excellent supplement to classroom learning about the Home Front. Many of the original fittings remain, including flushing toilets and a range of medical facilities.

The Finsbury Scheme

One of the most ambitious (but ultimately doomed) plans for air raid shelter construction was the proposal for a series of enormous deep shelters in the London Borough of Finsbury. Throughout the 1930s the construction of deep shelters was the cause of a great deal of political debate, particularly in dense urban working class communities such as Finsbury, where bombing was likely (and indeed proved) to be heavier than average, and where the influence of the Communist Party was strongest. In Finsbury the council decided to commission a study of deep shelter protection for the entire population, a highly ambitious proposal for which they commissioned the firm Tecton, run by the modernist architect Berthold Lubetkin and employing the brilliant civil engineer Ove Arup.

Arup's designs for the shelters were technologically advanced and meticulously crafted. He envisioned gigantic multi-storey structures in the form of flattened corkscrews dug into the ground, and constructed from the top down. Each would have multiple entrance points, air conditioning and a roof made of several layers of concrete many metres thick, interspersed with earth or sand layers to absorb the force of direct hits. In peacetime the shelters could be used as multi-storey car parks, and in the models that were exhibited at the time toy cars were placed around the edges as demonstrations.

The Finsbury deep shelter scheme attracted a great deal of publicity both within London and further afield. In particular it was noted that the proposed cost per head of population for the shelters, each of which could hold either around 7,500 or 12,500 people, was lower than for the tin-can Anderson shelters being distributed by the government. A government commission was set up to examine the issues of deep shelters that the scheme had raised, but ultimately ruled against them. The commission reached the absurd decision that to build such well protected shelters in poor areas risked creating a 'deep shelter mentality', which would cause the populace to cower in fear inside their shelters and refuse to emerge to work or fight. The stalwartness of the population in the face of the Blitz was to prove them badly wrong, but by then the damage had been done and the British population entered the war with a generally lower standard of air raid protection than Barcelona had achieved years before. All that remains of the Finsbury scheme are the plans that Arup created: astonishingly futuristic-looking designs that, had they been built, would have remained a fascinating part of Britain's wartime heritage and a boon for anyone hoping to park their car in central London.

Summary

Air raid precautions reached into the lives of every person in Britain during the Second World War. Even for those with no connection to the military or the war effort, there remained the fear of death from the air and the imperative to maintain the blackout and, when necessary, to take shelter in the air raid shelters. For the million and more who volunteered or worked as air raid wardens the routine of training, practice and preparedness led to action on the front line of the total war that brought violent death and destruction into everyday life. As the war came to an end, the wardens who had given up their days and nights – many of them also holding down full-time jobs – hung up their uniforms, tin hats and whistles. Wardens' posts were demolished or returned to their peacetime uses; air raid shelters were knocked down, sealed up or abandoned. The desires to move forward, forget the war and build the society of tomorrow were among the perfectly understandable reasons why the material heritage of air raid precautions was allowed to be swept away and forgotten. In any case, the forward-thinking person of 1945 might have thought, surely this material was so abundant, so uninteresting and so commonplace that no scholar would ever take an interest in it – after all, what did it have to do with the war?

Today archaeologists, historians and others studying the traces of the Home Front are fascinated with precisely this commonplace experience of war: while we honour 'the Few' of Fighter Command, we also want to understand the war experience of the many, the tens of millions whose war experiences made the modern nation. Gas masks were the everyday artefacts of this multitude, the air raid warden the familiar face of the war effort, and the air raid shelter a part of their daily or nightly routine. Studying these traces of everyday life in wartime opens up a wealth of historical knowledge: hundreds of thousands of extraordinary lives and stories.

As this chapter has shown, the heritage of air raid precautions is a vast resource for archaeologists to study — or for anyone interested in the Second World War. It is quite likely that you or someone you know will have traces of an air raid shelter in your garden, or buried in your local park. Hidden among family papers and heirlooms there might well be ARP badges or pamphlets, and even a gas mask or tin hat on top of a wardrobe or hanging in a shed. All of these things add to our understanding of Britain at war: none is without value or interest. Take care of them and pass them on.

Postscript: Health and Safety when Exploring Air Raid Shelters

Although they were originally built as places of safety, air raid shelters are not always the safest places to explore. Before gallivanting off to poke around the air raid shelter in your garden or local park, there are a number of things that should be borne in mind when planning your exploration as well as during it.

Structural integrity

Many shelters, particularly Andersons and some trench shelters with steel roofs, are likely to have been damaged by rust over the years. In some cases the covering of earth over the shelter – sometimes several tons – is held in place by the thinnest sheet of rusty metal. Even a small disturbance might send this crashing down to bury you. If in doubt, stay out, and inform the council – unstable structures might have to be demolished. During my most recent air raid shelter excavation the roof of a long-forgotten shelter in a nearby park collapsed unexpectedly, opening up a hole in the turf and necessitating its demolition and burial. Even concrete and brick structures may be unstable, and it's best to get them checked by a qualified surveyor or engineer before venturing inside.

Environmental hazards

Even structurally sound shelters present hazards. Many have been sealed for a long time, and the air inside can become dangerously stagnant. Many air raid shelters contain standing water, particularly if they were dug below the water table (as many were). Indeed, many Anderson shelters flooded as soon as they were installed, leading residents to abandon them altogether. Standing water presents a biohazard as well as a physical one.

Protective equipment

When the shelter is deemed safe to enter, it is still important to wear appropriate protective clothing and carry safety equipment. Hard hats and durable footwear are essential, and brightly coloured or reflective clothing are a good idea as well, although the latter can interfere with underground photography. In certain situations safety harnesses might be needed; these can be hired. If in doubt consult an expert.

Safety summary

The precautions for exploring air raid shelters are similar to those for caving or climbing. These include informing someone of your plans, and preferably not going off on your own. Even with all of these precautions, there are still risks involved in exploring air raid shelters. Through membership of Sub Brit or other organisations intrepid would-be explorers can learn safe practices from fellow enthusiasts. Finally, these safety tips are by no means exhaustive, and each situation must be assessed independently.

Further Reading

Brayley, Martin and Malcolm McGregor, *The British Home Front 1939–45* (Osprey, 2005)

Cooksley, Peter, *Home Front: Civilian Life in World War Two* (History Press, 2007)

Demarne, Cyril, *The London Blitz: a Fireman's Tale* (Parents' Centre Publications, 1980)

Doyle, Peter, *ARP and Civil Defence in the Second World War* (Shire, 2010)

Gregg, John, *The Shelter of the Tubes: Tube Sheltering in Wartime London* (Capital Transport, 2001)

Jappy, M.J., *Danger UXB: the Remarkable Story of the Disposal of Unexploded Bombs During the Second World War* (Channel 4 Books, 2001)

McCutcheon, Campbell (ed.), *Air Raid Precautions* (Tempus, 2007)

Saunders, Ann, *The London County Council Bomb Damage Maps 1939–1945* (London Topographical Society/London Metropolitan Archives, 2005)

Wade, Stephen, *Air Raid Shelters of the Second World War: Family Stories of Survival in the Blitz* (Pen & Sword, 2011)

Useful Websites

www.subbrit.org.uk

The website of Subterranea Britannica, the study group for manmade underground structures in the UK. The website includes photographs and reports of air raid shelters of all kinds around the country, and details of surviving sites that can be seen from the surface.

www.fortunecity.co.uk/meltingpot/oxford/330/mwindex.html

A site dedicated to the Civil Defence workers of Home Front Britain in the Second World War, providing a series of good, short overviews of the different services and their roles in the war.

Places to Visit

Stockport Air Raid Shelters

The mile of tunnels that make up the Stockport Air Raid Shelters have been restored to their wartime condition as a museum, with electric lighting, benches and bunks, and a first-aid station, as well as the original communal toilets. This is one of the best preserved and by far the best presented public shelters in Britain.

Stockport Air Raid Shelters
Chestergate
Stockport
SK1 1NE
www.airraidshelters.org.uk

Afterword

Archaeology is the study of people in the past, and the archaeology of the Second World War has revealed a great deal about the people of Britain in the six years of war that made the modern world. The everyday things pulled from bombsites, rubbish tips, buried air raid shelters and the seabed are reminders of these people: the millions of children whose lives were marked by living through the war; the millions more who served in the armed forces, worked in war industries or volunteered for civil defence; and the millions who struggled to continue with their everyday lives while the world burned.

Archaeologists studying the Second World War have a number of responsibilities that make up our ethical codes and guidelines. We are responsible for studying and caring for the remains of the past in all their forms, to ensure that they are protected for the future or that, if they are lost, we have at least recorded them so that the information that they contain can survive. In this we bear a responsibility not only to the wider public but to the scholars of the future who will also want to study and understand the past. Alongside this responsibility to the people of the future, we also have a responsibility to the people of the past: the population of Second World War Britain whose lives we attempt to uncover. Unusually for archaeology, many of these people are still alive and as we work to uncover their heritage we can often benefit greatly from their knowledge. Equally we owe them the courtesy of sharing our knowledge with them, and making sure that our work maintains the dignity of the living – and the dead.

To return to the questions raised at the start of this book – what is Second World War archaeology for, and why is it important? Britain's wartime heritage is a vast and varying resource, and it serves many different purposes. It is an educational resource, something that teachers and students can draw upon to better understand history as well as to understand the modern world that history has made. Many of the excavations of Second World War sites that I have been involved in have made efforts to include young learners in the archaeological work so that they can see, touch and understand their heritage. Learning and education is not only for the young: everyone involved in an excavation or survey of a wartime archaeological site is learning something, from the site and from each other. Even those who lived through the war find that there are things that they can learn from talking about their experiences to archaeologists and historians.

As well as a route into education, Second World War archaeology can be a way of commemorating the war and its tens of millions of dead. Excavating is akin to remembering: in both cases we talk about digging down through layers to uncover the past. When we excavate a site where people were killed or injured, we have a duty to remember them and honour their memory. In some cases, such as aviation archaeology, it is not unknown to find the remains of the dead during excavation, often of people who were reported as missing and who never received a proper burial. To recover a body, subject to legal and ethical restrictions, and to return it to the family is one of the most important functions of Second World War archaeology. Wherever possible and appropriate, archaeologists honour the memories of the people whose traces we uncover and preserve.

What is the future of Second World War archaeology? In the next twenty years the war will begin to slip over the edge of living memory, and there will be fewer and fewer people alive who can share their memories of the conflict. As the memories fade away, the material traces of the war – its archaeological heritage – will take on an ever-more important burden to tell the stories of the war. Currently we are in the era of 75th anniversaries of the various points of the war years: by the time we begin to reach 100th anniversaries the history and the archaeology will be very different, in ways that we cannot even imagine.

For now, most of the work described in this book is likely to continue. Aviation archaeologists will carry on excavating the remains of wartime aircraft from mountain tops and sea-beds; others will continue recording surviving wartime structures and buildings, including bunkers, air raid shelters, gas decontamination centres, air raid wardens' posts and their ilk. Excavators will continue to unearth the traces of bombed buildings, defensive sites, old airfields, prisoner of war camps and other civil and military sites. Some of this work will be driven by commercial imperatives as sites are cleared for development; some will be driven by personal curiosity and a desire to better understand the past. At the time of writing, English Heritage is piloting a scheme to record the archaeological remains that are routinely brought to the surface by fishing trawlers off the coast of Britain. The archaeologists responsible for this scheme have noted that among the heritage on the seabed, which dates from the Mesolithic through to the present, there are huge numbers of Second World War remains, including hundreds of wrecks and the remains of around 13,000 aircraft. Even as I was finishing this book a team of Royal Navy bomb disposal divers were carefully excavating the tail section of a V2 ballistic missile that had been found in Harwich harbour by members of a local sailing club. After ascertaining that the one-ton high explosive warhead was no longer in place, the divers recovered the missile's tail, including parts of the propulsion system, and brought them back to land to be displayed. On this basis, and the hundreds of similar stories that continually crop up, it is tempting to suggest that a large part of the future of Second World War archaeology lies beneath British waters.

As the wartime generation passes away, tiny personal traces of the war will be left behind: ration books and identity cards, service medals, gas masks, military buttons and badges, souvenirs and personal effects. Many of these will be common and everyday reminders of the war; a few will be rare and extraordinary. But all have stories to tell, and once their owners have gone it falls to archaeologists and historians to unravel these tales from the traces that remain. As for me, I plan to carry on excavating air raid shelters.

Further Reading

Bird, Christopher, *Silent Sentinels: the Story of Norfolk's Fixed Defences in the Twentieth Century* (Larks Press, 1999)

Burridge, David, *20th Century Defences in Britain: Kent* (Brassey's, 1997)

Carman, John and Patricia Carman, *Bloody Meadows: Investigating Landscapes of Battle* (History Press, 2006)

Carvell, Steve, *Twentieth-Century Defences in Warwickshire* (NPI Media Group, 2007)

Hegarty, Cain and Sarah Newsome, *Suffolk's Defended Shore: Coastal Fortifications from the Air* (English Heritage, 2007)

Jones, Colin, Bernard Lowry and Mick Wilks, *20th Century Defences in Britain: the West Midlands* (Logaston, 2008)

Lynch, Tim and Jon Cooksey, *Battlefield Archaeology* (History Press, 2007)

Osborne, Mike, *20th Century Defences in Britain: Cambridgeshire* (Concrete Publications, 2001)

Osborne, Mike, *20th Century Defences in Britain: The East Midlands* (Concrete Publications, 2004)

Osborne, Mike, *Defending Britain: Twentieth-Century Military Structures in the Landscape* (History Press, 2004)

Osborne, Mike, *20th Century Defences in Britain: the London Area* (Concrete Publications, 2007)

Osborne, Mike, *20th Century Defences in Britain: Norfolk* (Concrete Publications, 2008)

Osborne, Mike, *20th Century Defences in Britain: Suffolk* (Concrete Publications, 2008)

Osborne, Mike, *Pillboxes of Britain and Ireland* (History Press, 2008)

Pollard, Tony and Neil Oliver, *Two Men in a Trench: Battlefield Archaeology, the Key to Unlocking the Past* (Michael Joseph, 2002)

Schofield, John, *Modern Military Matters* (Council for British Archaeology, 2004)

Photo Credits

Plate 2:   Photograph by James Dixon, used with permission.

Plate 9:   Photograph by Simon Burchell, http://commons.wiki-media.org/wiki/File:Shalford_NT_World_War_II_pillbox_2.JPG

Plate 10: Photograph by Gaius Cornelius, http://commons.wiki-media.org/wiki/File:Spigot_mortar_emplacement,_Elvetham_Heath.JPG

Plate 11: Photograph by Gaius Cornelius, http://commons.wiki-media.org/wiki/File:Pillbox,_Octagonal,_Winchfield,_Pale_Lane_(south_east).JPG

Plate 12: Photograph by Andy Brockman, used with permission.

Plate 13: Photograph by Palmiped, http://commons.wiki-media.org/wiki/File:Muckleburgh_Collection.JPG

Plate 14: Photograph by Nathalie Cohen, used with permission.

Plate 16: Photograph by Nathalie Cohen, used with permission.

Plate 17: Photograph by Clem Rutter, http://commons.wikimedia.org/wiki/File:Thames_Richard_Montgomery_KC_7722_(Modified).JPG

Plate 24: Photograph courtesy of *Hertfordshire Mercury*.

Plate 28: Photograph by Vespasean, http://commons.wikimedia.org/wiki/File:Ludhamtower1.jpg

Plate 29: Photograph by Ivor the Driver, http://commons.wiki-media.org/wiki/File:RAF_Waltham_B1_Hangar.jpg

Plate 31: Photograph by Nick Catford, used with permission.

Plate 33: Photograph by Nick Catford, used with permission.

Plate 38: Photograph by Nick Catford, used with permission.

Index